Two Years

Life as a sixteen year old in a Japanese Prisoner of War Camp 1943 – 1945

by

Elizabeth van Kampen with Cecil Lowry

Copyright © 2015 Elizabeth van Kampen with Cecil Lowry

All rights reserved, including the right to reproduce this book, or portions thereof in any form. No part of this text may be reproduced, transmitted, downloaded, decompiled, reverse engineered, or stored, in any form or introduced into any information storage and retrieval system, in any form or by any means, whether electronic or mechanical without the express written permission of the author.

ISBN: 978-1-326-26724-7

PublishNation, London
www.publishnation.co.uk

This book is dedicated to

Theo and Cobie van Kampen

My wonderful parents

Contents

Introduction

Prologue

Chapter 1 Early Life

Chapter 2 World War Two Breaks Out

Chapter 3 The Japanese attack Pearl Harbour and British Malaya

Chapter 4 The Japanese Invade the Dutch East Indies

Chapter 5 The Pig Basket Massacre

Chapter 6 My Father is interned

Chapter 7 Guests of the Japanese

Chapter 8 My First Job and Tenko

Chapter 9 Goodbye to the little boys

Chapter 10 Freedom at last and Farewell Indonesia

Chapter 11 My father is dead

Chapter 12 A Career, a Husband and Travel

Chapter 13 In Search of my Father's Grave

Chapter 14 Demonstrations in The Hague and Reconciliation in Japan

Conclusion

Epilogue

Introduction

Sometimes as an author you spend days agonising over a suitable topic for your next book and suddenly one just drop's into your lap. This book falls into the latter category. As my father had been a Far East Prisoner of war, my interest has always been on the Japanese invasion of most of South East Asia during 1941/42 and the subsequent imprisonment of thousands of military and civilians until the end of the war in August 1945. Whilst researching the subject, I stumbled upon the website of Elizabeth van Kampen, a Dutch lady, who as a sixteen year old girl was imprisoned by the Japanese on the island of Java for two years. I realised that her story just had to be told.

We are often told that childhood is usually the happiest time of our lives, but in Elizabeth van Kampen's case, a blissfully happy childhood up to the age fourteen soon turned into a nightmare. For almost three years she experienced hunger, terror, violence, deaths of friends and eventually that of her own beloved father. In December 1941 Elizabeth was a bright, cheerful fourteen year old Dutch girl living with her parents and two sisters in Sumber Sewu on the beautiful island of Java in the Dutch East Indies. Whilst the Nazis had Europe in turmoil, the van Kampen family celebrated Christmas and were still enjoying an idyllic lifestyle on the rubber plantation where Elizabeth's father was manager. In a matter of months however, their lifestyle was about to change dramatically. On the 7 December 1941, in pursuit of their expansionist aims in South East Asia the Japanese bombed the American fleet at Pearl Harbour, whilst almost simultaneously launching a large invasion force into Siam (now Thailand) and the British Colony of Malaya. In less than 100 days Malaya and the supposedly impregnable fortress that was Singapore had fallen to the invaders. The Japanese noose was now closing in around the Dutch East Indies. On 28 February 1942 the Japanese invaded Java and eight days later the Dutch government on the Island surrendered. Across the Dutch East Indies some one hundred and seventy thousand civilians were soon to be incarcerated in Prisoner of War camps, of which some twenty five thousand died in captivity. Initially family life went on pretty much the same as it had been before the invasion for the van Kampen family. Although food was becoming scarce, Elizabeth's father Theo van Kampen as manager of a rubber plantation was a useful asset to the Japanese war effort and for the moment they were left alone to get on with their lives. They were well aware that many of their fellow compatriots had already been interned in prison camps all over the island, and as such were constantly under the threat of internment. The Japanese policy of interning Dutch nationals had been going on since the surrender and it was only a matter of time before the van Kampens were to lose their freedom. At the beginning of February 1943, along with many other Dutch nationals, Theo van Kampen was taken away from his family to an all male internment camp leaving Elizabeth's mother alone to look after the three girls.

For the next two years the van Kampen family were subjected to unspeakable horrors and deprivations at the hands of a most cruel and barbaric enemy. The Japanese were no respecters of race or sex and treated the Dutch men and women with contempt and hatred. Food was scarce to almost non existent and Elizabeth was forced to work long hours under appalling conditions, all made worse by the uncertainty about their beloved father.

When the Japanese surrendered to the allies in August 1945 after the Hiroshima and Nagasaki atomic bombings, Elizabeth along with her mother and sisters were free once again and returned to Holland, but without their father. The van Kampens were desperate to obtain news about him but it was not until January 1946 that they learnt he had died of dehydration in an internment camp on 25 March 1945 - a mere six months before the Japanese surrendered. On returning to Holland, the van Kampens experienced the increasingly negative way that Dutch colonialism had been portrayed in the mother country. They were verbally abused as rich freeloaders who had an easy ride whilst the Dutch people had endured six years of oppressive Nazi rule. She was called 'the daughter of a nasty exploiter, a slave driver, from the Dutch East Indies', along with many other vicious and hurtful things. Fifty years later Elizabeth went back to Indonesia in search of her father's grave and to try and find out why he was killed by the *Kempeitai* and in 2000 she visited Japan. Despite her harrowing experiences during WW2 she harbours no lasting bitterness towards the Japanese. I have no doubt in my mind that this lady is part of a large group of heroines who stoically refused to give in to the Japanese during those terrible years. This is her story.

Cecil Lowry

Prologue

Our memories of the past dim as the years go by and they often may not be accurately recorded. It is not my intention in this book to mislead or to hurt my readers but the events that follow are based on the memories of my experiences during those harrowing three years. To the best of my knowledge, they are historically correct and these things did actually occur. I make no apologies for outlining the cruelty inflicted by the Japanese on innocent civilians during that war, nor to add to the suffering of many of those who even today are still struggling to come to terms with psychological or physical problems arising from their incarnations.

During the first week of August 1945, we were given a little bit more and better quality food than was usual. The Japanese guards had become very quiet and left us alone for long periods. Something was definitely up. We were told that we had to stay in prison and were no longer required to go out to work. I was more than happy not to have to get up early and spend the day working but the downside was that we could not keep in touch with what was going on in the wider world.

On the twenty fourth of August, Mrs. Eichelberg our camp leader asked us all to gather outside where we were to be addressed by the camp commandant. 'Ladies, the war is over, you are now all free women, Japan surrendered to the Allies nine days ago and for some reason our guards have kept it to themselves until now', she announced calmly. We clapped and cheered and when a small group of women started singing the Dutch anthem the *Wilhelmus*, we all joined in. It was so uplifting to once again be singing our national anthem after two years of hell in this dirty, smelly prison. I still could not believe that my ordeal was finally over. Of course now my thoughts now turned once again to my father. Surely he would soon come to find us and we would be reunited as a family again. Little did I know that I was never to see him again.

Elizabeth van Kampen

Chapter 1

My Early Years

Theo van Kampen was born on 13 December 1898, in Helmond North Brabant, a district in the Southern Netherlands. In 1916 at the age of 18 he was required to undertake military service in the Dutch Army and was posted to the town of *Delft*, eleven kilometres south of The Hague. With World War One still raging across Europe, the Dutch Army was still on high alert despite the country remaining neutral.

A year after the end of the War he obtained a position working for KPM, a Dutch shipping company based in Amsterdam. KPM had a base in the Dutch East Indies where they maintained the connexions between the Islands. Two years later Theo was sent out to their office in Batvia at the age of twenty two.

The Dutch East Indies was formed as a colony of the Netherlands in 1800 when the Dutch East India Company was nationalised. By the early 1900's it was producing 20% of the world's coffee and tea, significant amounts of rubber and coconut along with most of the world's quinine, ironically a substance that as POWs, we were to be deprived of by the Japanese.

The Dutch East Indies were known as 'the girdle of emeralds' comprising thousands of islands stretching out over an area that, if projected onto a map of Europe would run from Ireland deep into Russia.

My father fell in love with the country right away and spent the next five years working hard and studying to improve his qualifications. He often travelled back to The Netherlands to sit his examinations. In 1925 he travelled back to sit an exam in Utrect, where on arrival in the city he found temporary accommodation in a house on Neude twenty six. In the lounge he met a pretty young Dutch woman called Cobie Kossen. It was love at first sight for the two young people, so Theo decided to stay in Holland and not return to the Dutch East Indies. By June the following year Theo and Cobie were married, the couple settling down in Helmond. Ten months later on 16 April 1927, I entered the world. Holland had been badly hit by the great depression of 1928/29 as did most other European countries and my father once again started to look for employment in the Dutch East Indies. Twenty months later he obtained a position as technical advisor to the rubber and coffee plantation of Suban Ajam in the settlement of Benkoelen. The van Kampen family set off in November 1928 on board the SS *Prins der Nederlan*, for what was to become for me 'a paradise on earth.

S.S. "Prins der Nederlanden"　　　　　　Stoomvaart Maatschappij "Nederland"

It took the ship a month to get to Batavia the capital of the Dutch East Indies, where we were then transferred to a smaller vessel that took us to Sumatra, the sixth largest island in the world.

On Sumatra houses were usually built on stilts and one of my earliest memories was crawling underneath the house to hide, an activity that was not without its dangers as there were some quite dangerous snakes, scorpions and other unpleasant creatures lurking there. It took some time to get to sleep at night because of the noises of the crickets, the shrieks of the birds and the screeches of the *Boedungs* (monkeys). Mother was constantly cleaning around the house as the warm damp climate resulted in mould forming very quickly and then of course there were the droppings of the many insects to be cleaned up.

My sister Henny was born in Benkoelen on 11 December 1930. Conditions on the Island were quite primitive at that time and mother was taken to a small hospital where a drunken Dutch doctor was waiting. The birth was straightforward but the local nurse was unable to cut the umbilical cord, so my father had to do it for her. I was now nearly four years of age now and it was wonderful to have a baby sister to look after and play with.

Playing in the garden of out home in Suban Ajam in 1932

The tropical climate was wonderful with lots of sunshine and the occasional heavy rainstorm. There are twelve hours of daylight and twelve hour of darkness all year round and at six pm; darkness falls in a matter of minutes. In Holland people talked about the weather on a daily basis but here it is just the same each day. It was great for swimming and when I was four years old I pestered my father to teach me to swim. He got tired of my pestering and one day said to me 'so young lady you want to swim, then you shall swim'. He promptly picked me up and threw me into the water next to my uncle, who was staying with us at the time. From that moment onwards I just loved swimming.

The next three years of my life were idyllic, living in that wonderful country and climate, but unfortunately this was not to last as we had to leave Sumatra in 1934. The world economy was in a deep depression and the plantation Suban Ajam where my father worked had to close down, leaving him looking for another job. He quickly obtained one in Batavia but as my mother was an only child and was missing her parents very much, we went back to Holland to see them for a while leaving my father on his own. We went by ship to Batavia and had to stay in a hotel for a few days until it was time for us to leave. When we left my father on the quayside we were all in tears, it felt as though the family was being broken up. It was my first experience of grief as my father disappeared into the distance.

Our grandparents were delighted that we had come home and were there to meet us when we arrived in Rotterdam. For the first five months we lived in The Hague with my grandparents and I was sent to a school in the city. It was horrible and a real culture shock as I found the children very different from those I had known back in the Dutch East Indies. Although I spoke fluent Dutch, they found my accent hard to understand and of course I was quite tanned from the tropical sunshine.

Five months later, we moved back to live with my other grandparents in my father's home town of Helmond. They had a beautiful big house with a garden, many fruit trees, a vegetable plot and a henhouse but unfortunately there were no banana or coconut trees.

My granddad took me to the same school that my father, aunts and uncles had all attended.

We stayed in Holland for ten months before packing our bags again and setting off to rejoin our father in Batvia. Both sets of grandparents were at the quayside to wave us off and I loved them all, especially grandfather van Kampen. 'Please come and visit us soon grand-dad' I said. 'Of course I will Elizabeth, and I will bring grandma as well' he replied. Unfortunately he died of a heart attack in 1937, before he was able to keep his promise. It was a sad moment when I learnt of his death.

We travelled back to the Dutch East Indies on the MS *Sibbajak*, a twelve thousand ton motor passenger liner built in 1927 for Rotterdam Lloyd. The journey took four weeks and as I celebrated my eighth birthday on 16 April whilst at sea, my mother arranged for a party on board, a party that was to last the whole journey. I remember getting lots of attention and lots of lovely presents. One evening just as the sun was going down, as Henny and I were looking through the porthole from our cabin we saw the bright lights of a big city twinkling in the distance; it looked beautiful with lots of small boats flitting around the harbour. Mother told us that it was the British colony of Singapore and that we would soon be approaching Java.

Two days later we arrived in Jakarta and caught a train to Bandung, the capital of West Java and the country's third largest city. Bandung is some ninety miles south east of Jakarta and my father had booked two rooms for us in a hotel there.

The next day we travelled by car the fifteen miles or so to the coffee and rubber plantation at Batu Lawang, where my father worked and had a house ready for us. Mother was delighted with our new home and father was happy to have his family back again. I never felt happier.

I was dismayed however when my father told me that I would have to go to a boarding school in a town called Tasikmalaya, some seventy miles away. There was no school in the neighbourhood and I was to stay with a Dutch family called Stam. Mr Stam was the headmaster of the school but he was not a particularly nice man and neither was his wife. I didn't understand much of what he was saying and he had a vicious temper. Mrs Stam often spanked me for the slightest thing; she also spanked her own two daughters Truusje and Tineke.

Fortunately I was able to go home every second weekend which was wonderful as I missed my parents and the home cooking of our Sundanese cook so much. He made the most delicious meals including cakes and sweets for Henny and I, and also taught us a few words of Sundanese, the main language of West Java.

One day my father announced that he was being promoted and transferred to a bigger and more important plantation over 500 miles away, near Malang in East Java. Of course I was delighted that I would be leaving that awful school I hated so much. It was January 1936 when we finally packed up our belongings and left by train from Tasikmalaya. It was an exciting journey to Malang and I just loved the sounds and the smells coming from the locomotive as we chugged along through beautiful scenery.

We passed though many small villages and towns where Indonesian children waved at us and we waved back from the train windows. The country was very lush and green and as we approached Malang I became very excited with the thought of seeing our new home. On arriving in the city we went straight to the Hotel Splendid where father had booked rooms and we had a lovely meal before Henny and I were sent to bed.

The next day we had a look round the city and I gazed in wonderment at the three volcanic mountains called the Semeru, the Arjuno and the Kawi that overlook it. It was love at first sight for me in this 'town in the mountains'.

Father left us the following day to start his new job on the coffee and rubber plantation Tretes Panggung, high up on the ridge of the *gunung* (volcano) Semeru. We were to stay in the hotel for a few more days until all our furniture arrived, but unfortunately that same afternoon Henny took ill and had to be taken to the hospital where it was discovered that she had bacterial dysentery. Mother was told that she might have to stay in the hospital for up to two weeks, so we had no alternative but to settle down and wait for her to get better. Fortunately five days later she was well enough to come out of hospital and we were able to set off for Panggung, where father was waiting for us.

Our new house was very nice and Sawilla, our new cook had tea and *kue kukus*, a sort of Indonesian steamed cake, waiting for us when we arrived.

The next day we all went to meet my father's employer Mr Houtsmuller who lived nearby with his wife and their five children. Their youngest daughter Agnes was to become my best friend and as you will read, we went back on a nostalgic visit to Indonesia together fifty years later. After my bad experience of school in Tasikmalaya I was a bit concerned as to whether I would like my new school in Malang, but I needn't have worried as it was delightful. I had a really nice understanding teacher and many friendly classmates.

We played together in the streets and spent many happy hours visiting each other's houses, where doors were always left wide open. As school started at seven in Java at that time, every Monday morning just before dawn, my father would drive me from our home to Dampit, a small town higher up on the mountains from where I caught a bus to Malang. After her bout of bacterial dysentery Henny was not yet strong enough to go to school so mother taught her at home until she was strong enough to go. The rest of 1936 seemed to pass very quickly and as 1937 dawned we entered quite a significant year. Our dear grandfather died, mother fell pregnant again and I reached double figures - I was now ten years old. Mother announced that the van Kampen family was to be expanded to five and of course Henny and I were delighted with this wonderful news. We just hoped that we would get a little brother.

Mother gave birth in the Lavalette Clinic on 20 December 1937 and I was taken straight to meet my new baby sister. Whilst I was disappointed not have the brother I wished for I took one look at my baby sister and fell in love with her right away. 'What are we going to call her?' I asked my mother. 'Jansje' she replied happily. It was the most wonderful Christmas present the van Kampen family could have been given. We were a very happy family, living in a beautiful part of the world and made even happier when my mother played the piano. She was an excellent pianist and Henny and I would sit in chairs next to her whilst Jansje slept in her cot. We would also listen to a lot of American music on the radio. The rest of 1938 was a wonderful time for us all, we lived in a beautiful part of the world, I loved my school, had a best friend in Agnes and two adorable sisters. Towards the end of that year my father was offered a new post on a coffee and rubber plantation in a place called Sumber Sewu, which means 'thousand wells'. It was almost 400 miles away and as it was again a promotion for him, he was very excited about taking up his new post. Mother had already seen the house we were to move into and she was also looking forward to the move. Initially I was not happy to leave my wonderful school and my friend Agnes, but I knew that it was a better job for my father so I happily accepted it. When we drove from the main road onto the driveway of our new home I couldn't believe my eyes - it was just beautiful. There was a big pond in front of the house surrounded by a huge garden and everything looked so green. I looked at my father with tears in my eyes: 'how beautiful' I said.

The van Kampen girls, taken in the garden at Sumber Sewu just before the outbreak of war in 1942

Chapter 2

World War Two Breaks out

Life was idyllic for a twelve year old girl living in Sumber Sewu in 1939, but before too long world events were to change our lives dramatically. Back in Europe on 1 September Nazi Germany invaded Poland. Five German armies made up of 1.5 million men, 2,000 tanks and 1,900 modern aircraft, quickly crushed less than a million Polish troops. It was an uneven contest and within five days German forces had occupied all of the frontier zones. By 8 September the Polish capital Warsaw had fallen and by 17 September the whole of Poland was in Nazi hands. This invasion provoked a global conflict as Britain and France then declared war on the Germans. On 10 May 1940, the Germans invaded the Netherlands causing Queen Wilhelmina and Prince Bernard to flee to England. The Dutch were ill-prepared to resist such an invasion and it was a great shock to all the Dutch people living so far away from their mother country. A feeling of deep sadness fell on the Dutch population in the Far East, but the sun continued to beat down on our little bit of paradise and to us children the occupation of Holland seemed like a world away. The Netherlands had hoped to remain neutral as they had done during the First World War twenty five years earlier, but Hitler ignored the plea and with his eyes on the strategic port of Rotterdam, he invaded the country with his superior forces. The Dutch government's attitude towards war was reflected in the state of the country's armed forces at that time. Holland had not significantly expanded her military since before the First World War and was inadequately armed for the Nazi assault. The world was about to change and the van Kampen family lifestyle was soon to change with it.

Christmas 1939 was looming, and of course December was always a busy month in our house. First there was *St Nicholas* day on 5 December, then Henny's birthday on the eleventh, then Jansje's birthday on the twentieth and then of course Christmas followed by the New year celebrations.

At school in Malang we celebrated *St Nicholas* day, the primary occasion for gift-giving, as was traditional in all Dutch schools. *St Nicholas* is supposedly the patron saint of children and the young children would put their shoes in front of the chimneys and sing *Sinterklaas* songs. They often put a carrot or some hay in the shoes, as a gift to *St. Nicholas'* horse and the next morning they would find a small present in their shoes. On the evening of 5 December, *Sinterklaas* brings presents to every child who has behaved well over the past year. On 8 February 1940, the Chinese New year started with a delicious prepared suckling-pig given to my parents by the Chinese shopkeeper at Sumber Sewu. Later on in the evening we watched a wonderful firework display and we were all allowed to stay up late to enjoy the celebrations. Two months later I became a teenager and Rasmina, our cook, made me the most wonderful maize cookies. I got lots of presents including my first watch and several very interesting books.

At Prince Bernhard's request the people from the Dutch East Indies set up a Spitfire fund to raise money to build new planes to assist with the defence of Europe from the Nazi invaders. Many people in Java donated a whole month's salary to this fund and even the local Indonesian population chipped in. We were also asked to donate metal and many families gave some of their pots and pans along with old tools to the fund. These were all collected up and transported to Batvia to be shipped back to England.

At Sumber Sewu the head-foreman Karto, came to my father with a small bag full with cents from the workers on the plantation.

'For our Queen', he said.

My father was touched by this wonderful gift from people who had so little and yet could still be so generous and who saw Queen Wilhelmina as their Queen as well. At school the war was discussed on a regular basis. We were able to keep up to date by listening to radio broadcasts and by reading the newspapers, but as children it seemed a long distance away, although we did worry about our friends and relatives back in Holland.

My mother would write to her parents in Holland every week and they would almost immediately write back, but when the war broke out she received no letters back. We had no means of knowing as to whether the letters got to them and we became really worried about the situation back in our homeland. Jansje was growing up fast now and loved to talk to Henny and I when we came home from boarding school for the weekend. She was lonely during the week and really pleased when her two big sisters came home. With the situation in Europe looking bleak, my father was called up for military training with the land-forces in Malang. By the autumn of 1940, the news coming through on the radio and in the newspapers was even more dismal. On 7 September 1940 Hitler's Luftwaffe began an intensive bombing campaign against British cities and industries. London was bombed on fifty-seven consecutive nights between 7 September and 2 November 1940 and the capital experienced further heavy raids during December. Fifteen other British cities were also subjected to major bombing attacks and some like Coventry, suffered extensive damage. Over 41,000 British civilians were killed and 137,000 injured during what was known as the Blitz on 27 September 1940, Germany Italy and Japan signed the Tripartite Pact in Berlin. This military alliance of the Axis powers was to try and discourage the United States from taking a more active involvement in the war in Europe. In South East Asia meanwhile, Japan was beginning to rattle its sabre. It had been almost ten years since they had invaded Manchuria and set up the puppet state of Manchukuo. Full scale war with China broke out six years later in 1937 after a minor military engagement at the Marco Polo Bridge. A Japanese regiment had been conducting night manoeuvres near the bridge and during a break, several shots were fired at them. Using this as an excuse the Japanese advanced upon the Chinese fort of Wanping and started shelling it resulting in an all out war. The United States had been putting pressure on the Japanese since they had annexed Manchuria and in 1940 they banned the export of oil to Japan. Since they had depended on the foreign imports of oil they started to cast envious glances at the Dutch East Indies and Malaysia, countries rich in oil reserves. It seemed as if a dark cloud was moving slowly towards the

Dutch East Indies and we were directly in its path. As children we could sense the worry amongst our parents.

Doctor Juda, a well-known surgeon from Malang, thought that it might be a good idea for the housewives living on all the plantations to go on a First Aid Course. My mother was more than happy to attend the course as often the Indonesians from Sumber Sewu would come to her for help when someone got hurt. She always felt so helpless when she could not do anything for them. On passing the test at the end of the course she received a certificate and a box containing some medicines, sterilized gauze and a thermometer and from that time onwards, the Indonesian residents of Sumber Sewu regarded my mother as their doctor. We celebrated Christmas 1940 in the usual van Kampen way, always tempered by the threat to our lives and jobs. By early 1941 the Japanese threat was becoming even more real with many Dutch people leaving Indonesia, mainly for Australia and South Africa. Rumours abounded that Indonesia was full of Japanese spies but the Japanese residents in Malang were still very polite as usual. My father's Japanese barber Mr. Matayoshi, still bowed to his clients as they entered his shop and the Japanese photographer in Malang was as polite and friendly as ever. After the war I learnt that Mr. Matayoshi was not only a barber but also a colonel in the Japanese army.

During the remaining months of 1941 more Australian, British and American troops began to arrive in our town, supplementing the Dutch garrison. The US Army Air Corps with their B17s were relocated to an airfield near Malang and we regularly saw them thundering overhead. We were now confident that we were well protected against any possible Japanese attack, an assumption that was to prove misguided as events were soon to prove.

At that time there were plenty of anti-Japanese jokes doing the rounds such as: 'They can never shoot straight, and will always miss because they are slit-eyed.' 'Their planes were made out of meat tins'. 'They can't run fast enough because of their crooked legs.' In the meantime however, the sun continued to shine down on the van Kampen family and Indonesia was still heaven on earth.

Chapter 3

The Japanese attack Pearl Harbour, invade British Malaya and the Dutch East Indies

On 7 December 1941 listening to our radio; we heard reports that the Japanese had attacked the main American Naval base at Pearl Harbour.

During the raid more than 2330 American service personnel were killed, with five of their eight battleships sunk and 188 combat planes knocked out. Fortunately the American aircraft carriers were at sea that day, thus preventing the almost complete annihilation of the fleet. Shortly after midnight on that same day the Japanese landed a large force on the east coast of Siam and in British Malaya. Under the command of General Yamashita the 25th Army was made up of 60,000 soldiers many of whom had gained experience in the war against China. He could also count on 3 Air Group, which had 459 aircraft and the Japanese Navy's Southern Command, which comprised of a battle cruiser, ten destroyers and five submarines.From their landing beaches the Japanese then flooded south-westwards towards the border town of Betong near Kroh and into Malaya. I learnt after the war that Air Chief Marshall Sir Robert Brooke-Popham, Commander in Chief Far East, had sent out a memo to all his commanders in the area at that time:

'Japan's action today gives the signal for the Empire's Naval, Army and Air Forces, and those of their allies, to go into action with a common aim and common ideals. We are ready. We have plenty of warning and our preparations are made and tested. We do not forget at this moment the years of patience and forbearance in which we have borne, with dignity and discipline, the petty insults and insolences inflicted on us by the Japanese in the Far East. We know

that those things were only done because Japan thought she could take advantage of our supposed weakness. Now, when Japan has decided to put the matter to a sterner test, she will find out that she had made a grievous mistake. We are confident our defences are strong and our weapons efficient. Whatever our race, and whether we are now in our native land or have come thousands of miles, we have one aim and one only. It is to defend these shores, to destroy such of our enemies as may set foot on our soil, and then, finally, to cripple the power of the enemy to endanger our ideals, our possessions and our peace. What of the enemy? We see before us a Japan drained for years by the exhausting claims of her wanton onslaught on China. We see a Japan whose trade and industry have been so isolated by these years of reckless adventure that, in a mood of desperation, her Government has flung her into war under the delusion that, by stabbing a friendly nation in the back, she can gain her end. Let her look at Italy and what has happened since that nation tried a similar base action. Let us remember that what we have here in the Far East forms part of the great campaign for the preservation in the world of truth and justice and freedom. Confidence, resolution, enterprise and devotion to the cause must and will inspire every one of us in the fighting services, while from the civilian population, Malay, Chinese, Indian or Burmese, we expect that patience, endurance and serenity which is the great virtue of the East and which will go far to assist the fighting man, to gain final and complete victory.'

The Dutch East Indies were now very much under threat. The next day, 8 December 1941, Queen Wilhelmina and the Dutch government declared war on Japan. Quite how we were going to wage such a war was unclear as Holland was by now under German control. Many people out in the Dutch East Indies now began to panic, whilst others were still optimistic that Japan could never win a war against the might of America, Australia and Great Britain. We heard that all the Dutch aircraft had been sent to Singapore to help with the defence of the Island, leaving us helpless against any sort of air attack. My father was one of the more optimistic ones, but of course he was naturally worried about the future for his wife and three daughters.

As the Japanese pushed the British and Australian forces down the Malay Peninsula we celebrated Christmas that year in a sombre mood. New Year came and went and in early January 1942 my father received an order from the Army in Malang to set up defensive positions around the plantations. He was also required to train some of the young Indonesians from Sumber Sewu to be part of the *Landwacht* (Home Guard), a task that he set about with relish as he always liked working with the local people. A supply of weapons and ammunition arrived for the defence which we kept in our house. The Army on the Dutch East Indies was over 100,000 strong with half being native Indonesians and the remainder made up of mainly Dutch civilians. Only five percent were regular trained troops. As we were now officially at war with Japan the Japanese population in the area were rounded up and put into internment camps. Some were even transported to Australia where they were interned until the end of the War.

The Japanese campaign against the *Dutch East Indies* commenced on 11 January 1942 when they landed a large force on the small island of *Tarakan*, off the coast of *Borneo*. They quickly overran the island with very little resistance and turned their attention to Borneo and Celebes on either side of the Macassar straits. Twelve days later, Japanese warships and transports were attacked by United States warships and Dutch aircraft. The Japanese suffered considerable losses but by the end of the month they had captured Borneo and Celebes quickly followed by Surabaya, the main naval base in the Dutch East IndiesEmperor Hirohito's mission was to expel all the European colonial powers from South East Asia, and to consolidate the entire East Asia into one entity, to be controlled again by a colonial power, this time an Asian one: Japan. He had embarked on what was called a 'maximum strength' colonial system that operated on new principles of man-subjugation, all out butchery and sexual servitude. We were all incredibly worried. On Saturday, 14 February 1942, my father came to take Henny and I home from our boarding-school for the weekend. We called at the bank in Malang and as we were leaving the premises we heard Japanese fighter aircraft flying overhead. Screaming low over the town the pilots proceeded to open fire randomly on the streets and as we dived for cover I saw two workmen fall from the roof of a building. Both men were left lying in a pool of blood and Henny and I were totally shocked, as was our father.

The following day, Sunday 15 February, we heard over the radio that Singapore had fallen into Japanese hands. In less than one hundred days Japanese forces had driven down the whole length of Malaya and taken the jewel in the British crown, a supposedly impregnable fortress. Speed was of the essence for the Japanese, never allowing the British, Indian and Australian forces time to re-group as they were forced into a full scale retreat. This was the first time the allied forces had come up against a full-scale attack by the Japanese and any thoughts of the Japanese fighting a conventional form of warfare were soon shattered. It had been confidently predicted that they would invade Singapore from the sea but the Japanese had other ideas and attacked down through the jungle and mangrove swamps of the Malay Peninsula. The British saw Singapore as their "Gibraltar in the Far East" and its loss was a bitter blow to morale in the East and demonstrated to the world that the Japanese Army was now a force to be reckoned with. On the 27 February one of the most significant naval battles of the war in the Far East took place, the Battle of the Java Sea. A Japanese fleet of forty transport ships and escorts were approaching Batvia when they were intercepted by a large British, Dutch and US force. In the fighting the Allies lost two light cruisers and three destroyers, as well as one heavy cruiser badly damaged and around 2,300 killed. Japanese losses numbered one destroyer badly damaged and another with moderate damage. Though soundly defeated, the Battle of the Java Sea, which lasted seven hours, is a testament to the Allies determination to try and defend the island at all costs. It was a resounding victory for the Japanese and effectively ended any meaningful naval resistance by the American, British, Dutch and Australian forces. Both sides suffered severe losses in the battle but the Japanese were able to land a large force one hundred miles east of Batvia and in less than a week they had taken the island. It seemed that we were now doomed. The Japanese 16th army landed 23,000 troops at three locations on the west coast of Java near Kragen on the night of the 28th February 1942. The main force landed near Merak with a secondary force landing near Eretan Wetan to the NW of Cheribon. Their main objectives were the cities of Batvia, Buitenzorg and Bandung and the Kalidjati airfield to the north, which they captured by the 1st March. The KNIL (Royal Netherlands East Indies Army) forces counter attacked to try and recapture the airfield but was driven back, with many men captured.

The Japanese troops that landed near the north-west tip of Java met only token resistance and it was only at Leuwilliang, to the west of Buitenzorg where Australian troops put up brave resistance. On the 5 March Batvia fell along with Buitenzorg the next day.

By 7 March, Bandung had fallen and the next day the KNIL surrendered to the Japanese Army at Kalidjati Military Airport, we were now in the hands of the Japanese. Three thousand Australian troops from the 7th Division, who had recently been brought back from the Middle East to help defend Java, were taken prisoner. General Wavell, commander of British troops in India, had warned that Java's defences would not hold out for more than a month. In the end it lasted a mere seven days. In the weeks leading up to the invasion senior Dutch Government officials, their family and personal friends were packed onto ships and sent into exile in Australia. There were still small groups of Australian, English and Dutch soldiers putting up resistance in the mountains in East-Java despite the fact that the Dutch East Indies government had surrendered. On paper the Dutch East Indies army was over one hundred thousand strong, with fifty percent native Indonesians and the other half mainly Dutch civilians recently mobilised into military service. When the Japanese started bombing, most of the Indonesian troops just disappeared back into the native population. The Japanese divided the DEI into three regions for administrative purpose. Sumatra was occupied by the 25th Army, Java and Madura by the 16th Army and Borneo by the Japanese Navy. Japanese aircraft were now flying overhead on a daily basis; it was a strange and somewhat unreal experience. The only Japanese people I had come across before were those living in Malang and they were always very polite and friendly towards us, but now they were our enemies. The

Japanese began rounding up and imprisoning all the prominent Dutchmen who they considered not essential in the running of the country. They used the telephone book to find out who they were as it listed the positions people held, such as judges, policemen, engineers and company directors and we feared that our father would soon be on the list. We were given advice by the local police as to how we were to behave towards our captors. 'Bow deeply every time you meet a Japanese man and switch off all lights at sundown' we were told. As women we were advised not to look into the eyes of the Japanese men, but to keep our eyes firmly fixed on their feet.

The following day Japanese soldiers entered Malang. Henny and I had our first sight of the soldiers from the recreation room in our school and we were appalled at the sight we saw. They looked terrible, dirty and unkempt, some were on bicycles, others were marching and they carried rifles almost a big as them. Most had a sullen, vicious look on there faces and looked ready to shoot at anyone who might pose a threat to them. Was this the all conquering Japanese Army that was to conquer most of South East Asia I wondered? My father felt that it was too dangerous for my mother and Jansje to remain with him at Sumber Sewu so he brought them to stay with Henny and I at our boarding-school, where small guestrooms were available.

With the situation uncertain we thought it better that we stay inside the school buildings, only the Indonesians working for the nuns felt confident going out to do the shopping for food.

A few days later the Japanese issued an order that all Dutch schools in Indonesia were to be closed down. Parents starting arriving to take their children home and suddenly the school felt empty and abandoned. We all felt sad as our happy schooldays were now over and our lives were soon to change dramatically. Dutch was now a strictly forbidden language. Fortunately we had a huge school library so we had lots of books to read to keep us occupied and take our minds off the invasion. For the time being we were left to get on with our lives the best way we could. Although we didn't know it at the time, civilian internment of Dutch nationals had started a matter of weeks after the surrender with most of the prominent people from government and industry imprisoned in Struiswijk prison, in Bandung.

Whilst we were left alone many men aged 17 to 60 were already being rounded up by the Japanese and taken to camps all over Java. The mass internment of women, children and older men began in October 1942 and we just lived one day at a time waiting to be taken from our home. A few weeks later my father decided that we should leave the school and all go back to Sumber Sewu. It was nice to be home again and to see Pa Min, Karto and the rest of our staff. There seemed to be absolutely nothing to fear on the plantation, the Indonesians were nice as ever to us and we didn't see any Japanese soldiers around.

Life began to feel normal again and I started to go out walking again with my father, often visiting the kampong (Indonesian township) nearby. I just loved to visit the kampong, where the sounds and smells were just exquisite. I was allowed to go out riding on my horse Trip, but was told to stay close to the house. The Japanese left us alone and we could move around freely, but we always had a sense that they were watching us wherever we went. As we were now under strict Japanese control, we were given a Japanese flag that we had to display in the garden at the front of our house. It became Pa Min's duty to run up the flag every morning and bring it down every evening just before the sun set, a task that he hated. One afternoon, Karto the head-foreman brought a man who had lost a finger, to the house. The poor man worked at another plantation where no one had the skills to help him but he knew that my mother would be able to help. She stopped the bleeding; put some tincture of iodine on it to ward off infection and then a bandage to keep it clean.

'How did this happen?' she asked the man. 'I stole some food and a Japanese soldier just chopped it off' he sobbed. An early indication of the cruelty we were soon to experience. By now my father, along with all the other Dutch, British, American and Australians living in Indonesia, was no longer receiving his salary. All bank accounts had been blocked and we were not allowed access to our own money. We existed on a small amount of money from the firm my father worked for, brought secretly from Surabaya to my father's boss and then to the employees on the plantations. With just a small amount of money to buy food we had to eat whatever was available.

We still had rabbits and eggs to eat and we still had an abundant supply of vegetables as my mother and Pa Min had planted seeds in the kitchen garden. As there were many fruit trees in the gardens we also had an abundance of beautiful fruit. Life was not too bad for the moment. We were now classed as foreigners living on Japanese territory and were required to pay for a *Pendaftaran*, the Indonesian word for a registration card. The cost in Japanese yen was the equivalent of 150 Dutch Guilders for men and 100 for women. The Japanese had already printed large amounts of their currency in advance of the occupation and every person over the age of eighteen had to pay this levy. Many people could not afford to pay in one lump sum so they were required to pay it off on a monthly basis. The *Pendaftaran* was supposed to keep us out of internment camps but in essence it was simply a tax, as events were soon to prove. We still had our radio that had been keeping us abreast of world affairs, but one day we had a visit from the Indonesian police. Under orders from the Japanese commanding officer they proceeded to seal off a part of the radio allowing us only a limited amount of stations. Dutch newspapers and magazines had already been closed down and the radio now only transmitted news in Malay or Japanese. We managed to open up the back panel and could change channels using a pair of pliers, enabling us to listen to the BBC World Service, but the resulting news was not particularly good. The Japanese had now taken most of South East Asia and were pushing up into Burma in the north and towards Australia in the south. Things were indeed looking very bleak but fortunately we still had our telephone and were able to keep in touch with our family and a few friends. Father was concerned that he might be taken away to an internment camp at any time and started taking photographs of the family for posterity. If he was to be taken away he wanted to have a family photograph with him and he was concerned that the Japanese might take away his camera. He had the photos developed at the local Chinese photographer's shop and asked him to keep copies in his archives in case the originals went missing. My father's concerns proved valid as a week later the Police called and took his camera away on the orders of the Japanese, along with our radio.

Chapter 4

The Pig Basket Atrocity

Father was working hard on the Plantation and training Karto his head foreman to take over from him if anything happened and he had to leave. Karto was a proud, loyal and hardworking Madurese who learnt fast and he had a deep respect for my father. One day towards the end of October 1942, as my father and I were walking back home down the main road from the plantation for lunch we heard the sounds of vehicles. As the vehicles were coming towards us we scrambled off the road and hid behind some bushes where we watched five trucks come round the bend. As they passed by a matter of yards from us we were both stunned by the sights and sounds emanating from them. The trucks were piled high with bamboo pig baskets containing not pigs, but crammed with screaming men. 'water, water, please', they screamed in Dutch and English. My father said softly 'oh my god, those poor men'. After they had passed we walked home without saying a word to each other. It was as though we had just emerged from a nightmare. Even today I can still hear those poor men crying and screaming for help and for water. Over lunch my father told my mother the whole story. She was also stunned and revolted and could hardly believe that human beings could do such things to each other.

It wasn't until nearly fifty years later I found out the full extent of the atrocities carried out by the Japanese, near Malang on that infamous day in 1942. After the Dutch East Indies surrendered, around two hundred Allied soldiers had taken to the hills, forming themselves into groups of resistance fighters. With so many Japanese forces in the region, they were eventually caught and squeezed into three foot long bamboo pig baskets. They were then transported in five open lorries, under a broiling 38 degree sun to the coast. Half dead from thirst and cramp the captives were carried on board waiting boats which then sailed out to the shark infested waters off the coast of Surabaya. There, the unfortunate prisoners, still enclosed in their bamboo cages, were thrown overboard to the waiting man-eaters. The commander in chief of Japanese forces in Java, General Imamura, was later acquitted of this atrocity in a Netherlands court for lack of evidence, but a subsequent Australian Military Court found him responsible and handed down a sentence of ten years imprisonment. At least some justice for the horrible sights my father and I witnessed that day. We were not the only people in the area to witness the start of this terrible atrocity; many people were called to give evidence at the war crimes tribunals in 1946. A thirty six year old Dutch lady Mrs L.M.C gave the following evidence:

'I am 31 years of age, Dutch, born in Surabaya of Dutch nationality. My present home is also in Surabaya. In the 2nd half of April or early May 1943, I was on my way to an estate near Dampit when I saw trucks coming out of a side road and turning on to the main road in my direction. This road in only 5 to 6 meters wide and the driver of my carriage stopped on the end of the road to let the trucks pass. From a distance of about 2 meters I saw that four trucks were loaded with baskets, stacked 3 and 4 high. In each basket was a man with his hands tied on his back and his legs drawn up and tied to his body with thick ropes. Some of the men looked Ambonnese, others were Europeans. They were in green, many torn up uniforms. The faces and bodies I saw were covered with blood. Their guards were Kempeitai soldiers. Another truck and several motor cycles with Kempeitai soldiers followed on. My mother and I heard later from Indonesians that the trucks first went to Ampelgading and from there along various estates roads back to the main road (the South Smeroe Road) and proceeded to Pasirian on the South Coast. I was told that the prisoners, alive and in baskets were thrown over the high cliffs into the sea at Pasirian at the spot where the ancient Indonesians had their place of sacrifices. The commandant in charge 1942/43 Kempeitai Malang provence, was a tall man, martial figure, broad shoulders, short straight hair, deep voice and an almost European. The local Kempeitai commander from Malang during 1942/43 MIIDA 9 nickname) The lion of Malang.'Signed Mrs. L.M. C. This day, 8 March 1946

Over the years I often thought to myself 'Did my father ever learn what happened to those poor men? Had any of the Indonesians also seen it? Did he speak with Karto about this tragedy?' Of course I shall never know the answer to these questions.

We expected a visit from the Japanese military at any time as they had already visited Wonokerto, the main plantation and other plantations in the area. It was only a matter of time before we too had a visit. A few days later my father received a phone call from the police in Ampelgading informing him that he was to take his car to the police station. Most of the Dutch staff on the other plantations had already lost their cars and he knew that he was about to lose his beloved Hudson to the Japanese.

I accompanied him in the car to the police station where he had to sign a letter in Malay and Japanese, agreeing to hand it over to the Japanese Army. We didn't even get a receipt, just a 'thank you' from the Indonesian police, and to make matters worse, we then had to walk home. When we got home everyone was crying. There was great sadness in the van Kampen house that day; we had lost our wonderful car. We heard that our Governor General Mr. Tjarda van Starkenborgh Stachouwer, along with other Dutch officials had been shipped to Formosa on board the Ake Maru, formally ending Dutch rule and leaving us even more depressed. I found out later that his American wife along with their daughter had not got out and were imprisoned along with the famous Hungarian pianist Lili Kraus. Apparently Lili gave concerts to the inmates of the camp she was interred in at Tangarang. Christmas 1942 was now upon us and as my mother was a good cook, she did her best in the kitchen to prepare a nice Christmas meal with the meagre resources at her disposal. The usual Christmas tree was missing and we had no decorations, only a few candles to brighten up the gloom. It was a sombre Christmas, but fortunately we still had our piano which mother played beautifully as we all sang carols before dinner. Just as we were about to start our Christmas dinner we heard Pa Min calling; 'orang Nippon, orang Nippon, Japanese coming'. Mother quickly took the food back to the kitchen and father went to the front door to greet the visitors.

Two cars pulled up and six or seven Japanese soldiers jumped out led by an officer. The officer was smartly dressed in a neat brown uniform and gleaming black boots. He had a gun strapped to his waist along with a long sword in a leather scabbard. The ordinary soldiers wore green uniforms, caps with stripes of white cloth at the neck and carried rifles with long bayonets attached. 'We have been ordered to search your house for weapons and if you have any hidden you should own up right away', he told us in broken English. 'I have no weapons' my father replied. The officer asked to see our papers and enquired as to how the plantation was performing. My father told him that it was doing well but that he still had a lot of work to do to keep it running smoothly. By saying this he hoped that he might avoid internment if he was deemed to be of some use to the Japanese. The soldiers then proceeded to search the house for weapons. They demanded that Pa Min get a ladder so that they could climb into the roof space. Unfortunately they were not aware of the fragility of the ceiling and one of them fell through onto the floor leaving a huge gaping hole in our ceiling. I wanted to laugh, but was frightened and worried about what might happen next. After around two hours of searching, the soldiers left the house leaving us to carry on with our Christmas dinner. We did our best to laugh and joke but little did we realize that this would be the last Christmas dinner that we would ever have together as a complete family. There were now very few Dutch or other European people who had not been interned and we were fearful that it was only a matter of time before we were taken away.

As 1942 drew to a close, fortunately we had no more Japanese visitors. Mother prepared a simple meal to bring in the New Year, once again a sombre occasion in the van Kampen household. We all hoped that 1943 would bring an end to the Japanese occupation of what we considered to be 'our country'. I often went out walking in the hills with my father and one beautiful day we climbed to the top of a small hill where we had the most superb views of the Indian Ocean. The ocean where it was reputed that 'Loro Kidul' the goddess from the ocean lives. She is a legendary Indonesian spirit, known as the Queen of the Southern Sea of Java and also the legendary consort of the Sultans of Mataram and Yogyakarta. As we gazed out over the ocean, my father looked at me and said; 'Elizabeth, I have to ask you something. As you are almost sixteen I want you to look after your mother and your sisters when I have to leave Sumber Sewu. Will you promise me that?' I was totally shocked by his request. 'I can't do that father' I replied. 'Yes, you can, you must promise me that you will look after them until this war is over and I will come back and join you again'. 'I will do my best, father' I said, with tears in my eyes.

Chapter 5

My Father is interned

It was the beginning of February 1943 when my father received a phone call from the police-station at Ampelgading. He was told that, along with his boss Mr. Sloekers, he was to leave Sumber Sewu within six days and catch a train to Malang and report to the Marine camp there. The moment we had been dreading for months was almost upon us and it was a sad six days leading up to his departure. He had arranged that we would get some money every month through Mrs Sloekers to provide us with food. He was calm as he packed his suitcase on the day he was due to leave, just as if he was going away for a few days on business. A *Dokar* (buggy) came to pick him up from the house and Karto, along with several other Indonesian foremen, had come to say goodbye. They wished him well and hoped that he would soon come back to Sumber Sewu. They were truly wonderful people. We kissed father goodbye and as the buggy pulled away there were tears in all our eyes. Henny started running after him shouting and crying out for him to stay. The van Kampen family were devastated. Mother phoned Aunt Miep to tell her that father was now interned at the Marine camp in Malang. Of course Uncle Pierre had already been interned in Kidiri camp at that time, and by now most of the Dutch men had been interned. The house without my father felt terribly empty and the implications of the pledge I had made to him up in the hills suddenly hit me. My life from that moment on was to get a lot harder. Life had to go on of course and mother put on a brave face, but every so often she would burst out crying and I tried my best to cheer her up even though I felt as bad as she did. A week later a post card written in Malay arrived from my father. We were all so excited and we gathered round as mother read it out. My mother kept this letter and I still have it to this day. Literally translated into English it reads:

To Mrs.C van KampenCD Wonokerto (Sumber Sewu was a department from Wonokerto) Dampit.

Dearest Cobie, Liesje, Henny en Jansje,How is everything at Sumber Sewu? How is it now with Liesje's eyes, still not better? That is a real problem. And Henny still too skinny, she has to eat well, lots of chicken meat and rabbit. Over here we have enough to eat, meat, bread, potatoes and meat. Also coffee and tea. Cobie, when you visited you brought such a lot, I will have enough for a whole month. There are many books over here, we have gramophone and I am learning to play chess. But I am thinking about you and the children all the time. Here for me there is enough. But how is it at Sumber Sewu? No problems? But when you do have problems then just come to Malang. On the other hand it is of course better for the children at Sumber Sewu for the weather is over there so good. Cobie, you must let me know if you need any money for I have enough but I am so worried that I can't help you. For myself there is enough even if I have to stay for a year long over here and I can also borrow. I have good friends over here. There are many fine men. Cobie did you already received some loan? I hope so for you must not come short of money.But luckily there is food enough. Up till now I wrote you five postcards and from you I received two.

Dearest Cobie, Liesje, Henny, Jansje receive many kisses and love from Theo, Paps.

We were all so relieved to learn that he was in good spirits and was being treated well and given reasonable food. Over the coming months we received several more postcards from him and I still have a second postcard he wrote almost two months later. From the two postcards I have gleaned that he wasn't too happy to only get seven cards from us as against the sixteen he wrote at that time:

Th.G.van KampenWijk commissieIdjenboulevard / Goentoerweg Marinekamp MALANG
Dearest Cobie, Liesje, Henny, Jansje How is everything at Sumber Sewu? It is quite a long time ago since I received a postcard from you. Over here everything is still okay. And how is it with Henny, can she walk a little bit better? Can you get enough good food? Here

there is enough and I do read many books. Every Sunday we have music. But all of it is very heavy classical music. Does Liesje do her best to play the piano? And how about the field? Becoming very nice I guess and then you will get lots of fruits. Just hoping that it altogether will be enough. If you are short of anything please write. I believe that you will come over here in 2 weeks time, but don't bring anything for me. Maybe just some peanut butter and some jam. And how about Cobie's teeth has there been something done about them? If you have some time while you are in Malang then please do something about it before it is too late. I have already written 16 cards and received 7 from you. I write twice a week now. Please give my greetings to Cora. Lots of love to Copie, Liesje, Henny, Jansje and receive many kisses from Paps, Theo.

It was almost a month before my mother was allowed to visit father in the camp. As it was such a long way she went to see him on her own leaving us with Mrs Sloekers. We were all disappointed and when she got back we were eager to hear about him. 'Your father is well and in good spirits, it's not too bad for him' she said. Naturally this made me feel better even though I was missing him so much.

I turned sixteen on 16 April and I received the best birthday present ever, my mother said that she would take me to see my father at last. Mother and I went by *dokar* to Dampit where we met Mrs Hoebregts whose husband was in the same camp as my father. They had decided to travel together for company. From Dampit we boarded a very crowded train for Malang and had to stand most of the journey, I was really looking forward to visiting Malang again as well as seeing my father. There were Japanese soldiers on the train and when Mrs Hoebregts spoke to my mother in Dutch, a soldier strode up to her and slapped her viciously across the face: 'You speak Malay or Japanese' he shouted in perfect English - our first taste of Japanese brutality. We got a buggy from Malang station to the Marine camp and as I was now 16 and considered an adult, I was not allowed inside the men's prison. Only children under sixteen years of age were allowed into the men's camps with their mothers and as I was now sixteen I had to speak to him from outside the camp gates. My father had to stand one metre inside the gates and I had to stand one metre on the outside of the gates. We were only allowed to speak for ten minutes in Malay, as Dutch was now a forbidden language. A guard stood next to us to check that we were not speaking our native language. 'We are all fine back at Sumber Sewu' I told him. The ten minutes of our conversation passed far too quickly and as he walked back into the camp I shouted 'Until the next time'. Little did he or I know then, that there would never be a next time as seven months later he was transferred to a Kempetei controlled prison. Mother was then allowed inside the prison with father and as they walked through the gates the tears started rolling down my cheeks.

Several days later my mother got a phone call from her friend Mrs Sloekers. 'I have just had a very polite and friendly Japanese visitor to my house and he asked me if I could play the piano for him. As you know I can't play the piano very well so I suggested you to him'. She told mother. 'He seems a nice man and he is on his way over to see you'. Mother was not at all pleased that Mrs Sloekers had not checked if it would be alright for him to visit and was angry with her.

A short time later, a car pulled up at the front of our house and a tall Japanese officer stepped out. Mother greeted him politely at the door and escorted him into the living room where she offered him a drink of lemon juice. 'Mrs Sloekers said that you are a good pianist and might play for me' he said in perfect English. 'I have been playing the piano since I was eight years old and I hope that I will never be parted from it' replied mother. The officer simply smiled and she started to play. He closed his eyes and hummed along to the music as mother went through several tunes. Every so often he would open his eyes and glance across at Henny, something that did get me a little worried.

When she had finished her repertoire, the officer stood up and applauded. 'You play very well Mrs van Kampen' he said. He then wrote down something in Japanese on a piece of paper and gave that to my mother. 'Take your daughter Henny to the Lavalette Clinic in Malang and hand over this note', he said. 'I'm a doctor and I think she may be ill as she does not look well and is very thin. The clinic will telephone to let you know when you should come', he added

He thanked her again for playing for him, stroked Jansje's hair, waved us goodbye and left us all standing at the door in a state of astonishment that a member of the Japanese invasion forces could be so friendly and helpful.

A week or so later mother got a phone-call from the Clinic asking her to bring Henny right away. When we arrived Henny was thoroughly examined and diagnosed with the start of rickets, through a lack of Vitamin D and calcium. They told us that they would be keeping her in for two weeks where she was to be given supplements and sessions of artificial sun light.

That kind Japanese doctor gave my sister a chance to get through the following two years and to this day we are indebted to him. I have often wondered over the years did that Japanese doctor know in 1943 what was in store for us. Did he know that we were going to suffer terribly, and that many Dutch children were going to die at the hands of his fellow countrymen though lack of food and medical help? We will never know, but I regret not asking him his name and I would now like to say: 'Thank you very much for your help Japanese doctor'.

Chapter 6

Guests of the Japanese

At the beginning of July 1943 we received the news that we had been dreading. We were to leave our home in Sumber Sewu, report to an internment camp near Malang and to take with us only what we could carry. I was devastated to be leaving behind our little white dog Molly and my horse Trip and was worried as to what would become of them. Mother suggested that I leave them with Karto's son. Of course Rasmina and Pa Min would now be out of work and would have to look for other jobs; it was to be such a sad time in all our lives. On 11 July our luggage was packed and we prepared to leave and it was one of the saddest moments of my young life when I put on my small rucksack and said goodbye to the staff. Tears streamed down my cheeks. Mother handed Karto the keys of the house as he stood respectfully to attention. '*Hormat (respect) to* Mrs and Mr Van Kampen', he said in a loud emotional voice.

All our Indonesian workers lined up and stood to attention as we were herded into a truck, an honour to our family that I shall never forget; it made a deep impression on me. 'Adieu beautiful Sumber Sewu, you are my paradise on earth'. We were all convinced that the move was only temporary as this tiny backward Japanese nation could not possibly last out against the combined might of British and American forces. 'You will be back home in time for Christmas' said one of my friends.

Four uncomfortable hours later we were deposited in front of a house on Welirang street 43 A, a street we all knew very well from previous visits. The area was now an internment camp called 'De Wijk' and the houses were surrounded by a high barbed wire fence with sentry-boxes located at intervals round the perimeter. These boxes were manned by Japanese or Indonesian soldiers and as we walked through the gates dozens of them stood spaced out several metres from the fence. They all seemed to be scowling at us and had long bayonets fixed to the top of their rifles. The camp was opened in mid December 1942 as a 'protected' neighbourhood near Merbaboe Park.

The camp De Wijk had been opened by the Japanese in mid December 1942 as a 'protected' neighbourhood near Merbaboe Park and housed around 7000 women, children along with a few older men. It was called 'a protection' camp,' because the Japanese thought that we needed protection from the Indonesian population. They were aware of the anti Dutch feelings among the Indonesians and felt that it was better if we were all in one camp. The commandant of the camp was a Japanese Colonel called Kato, assisted by guards who were mainly native police officers. Four uncomfortable hours later we were deposited in front of a house on Welirang street 43 A, a street we all knew very well from previous visits. The house to which we were allocated was already occupied by several families and we were given one room for the four of us. Whilst conditions were cramped, it was nice for us as we had several other Dutch families around to talk to. Hot water was very limited so we had to be careful not to use too much for a bath or to wash our clothes and cooking had to be done over a charcoal grill. The De Wijk camp was located in the Bergenbuurt (mountain) quarter of Malang and was one of the largest women's camps on Java. Fortunately we were allowed to go out of the camp to purchase food with what money we had left at the *'pasar'* (Indonesian market), where friendly Indonesian men and women sold fruit and vegetables.

A few weeks later however, when we arrived at the entrance to the *pasar* a large sign said closed. Gone were the friendly Indonesian women, gone was all that delicious Indonesian fruit and of course gone was our little bit of freedom. Now where were we going to get our fresh fruit and vegetables? With our money fast running out we now had to rely on the soup kitchen organised by the Japanese where we got one meal a day. To supplement this we had to buy the rest of our food in the camp shop at vastly inflated prices. Food was becoming scarce. Any form of religious service was banned as was any form of education including books, pens and paper, anything that might give us hope and keep our spirits up was quashed. Consequently life in De Wijk camp was boring and of course as children we were naturally explorative. One afternoon four of us decided to try and get into one of the empty houses in nearby Welirang Street. We knew that it was forbidden to go into these houses but as children, curiosity got the better of us so we took the risk. The house was just on the other side of the street from the Christian High School, a building that the Kempeitai had taken over as their headquarters. We tried all the doors to the house but as they were all locked we decided to explore the back gardens, playing hide and seek around the trees and bushes. We all froze when we heard the most chilling screams coming from the School building just across the street. We were very scared so we quickly scarpered. I learnt later that many people were tortured by the Kempeitai in that building and that is probably what we heard on that day in July 1943. As the weeks dragged by more and more people began to arrive at the camp. The atmosphere began to change as by now none of us had any money left and we were struggling to get enough food to eat.

The Indonesian milkman was no longer allowed to enter the camp; consequently there was no more milk or butter to be had. It was a dismal time.

It was one day in November 1943 when a male visitor called into the camp. He had been sent from the 'Marine camp' where our father was interned and brought with him some bad news. 'Your husband has been taken to the Kempeitai headquarters for questioning. They thought that he had hidden weapons and ammunition in your house at Sumber Sewu' he said to my mother. 'I have been sent to get you to sign these documents confirming that you don't know anything about any weapons', he added. We were well aware of the fearful reputation of the Kempeitai for torturing suspects and were now greatly concerned about our father. From that time onwards we heard no more news about father and we got no more letters from him. This was very unusual as he usually wrote to us on a regular basis. At the beginning of December 1943 we started to think about father's birthday on the 13th. It would be the first time that we had been separated for any one of the family's birthday and we knew that it would be a sad day. Mother did her best to cheer us all up and we all sang happy birthday to him in his absence.

Christmas 1943 came and went as did the dawning of 1944. It had now been two years since I saw the first Japanese troops marching into Malang. Rumours (which turned out to be true) were now flying around the camp that we were all about to be transported to Central Java and on 13 February, we were ordered to pack our meagre belongings and prepare to leave Malang. I was so sad to leave this beautiful mountain town and also to leave my father behind in a Kempeitai prison that I went and sat quietly in a corner. 'Adieu Daddy, adieu Malang'.

At Malang station we were herded into a dirty, smelly goods train. It was so crammed that we had to sit huddled together on the floor. There was no toilet on the train and we had very little food or water but fortunately mother had brought along some bananas, water and a toilet-pot. We had no idea where we were going and many of the small children cried for most of what was to be a very long hot journey taking twenty four hours. There was a terrible smell of sick and death that lingered in the air and people were crying and moaning in pain and misery. The train headed westwards and initially we thought that we might be heading for Jakarta. But by late afternoon the next day we arrived at Ambarawa in Central Java where six hundred and eighty Dutch women and children stepped out of that stinking train, happy at least to get some fresh air after having been cooped up for what seemed like ages. As we wearily gathered up our belongings in the hot afternoon sunshine, the Japanese military who were accompanying the group screamed at us and ordered us to climb into a fleet of trucks parked just outside the station. It was chaos and everyone was panicking about their luggage which had been dumped in a large pile on the ground. We managed to locate our cases but the four mattresses we had brought were nowhere to be seen. The guards told us that they were on the next train and that we would get them later. From Ambarawa central station we were driven on to Banyu Biru, a journey of around ninety miles over rough dusty roads with great clouds of dust thrown up by the wheels. By now we were all exhausted, tired, hungry and thirsty and the looks on the faces of the women and children were of utter apprehension and confusion. Bored and listless Japanese guards sat on either side of the tailgates with their rifles propped between their knees. As we bumped along lots of young Indonesians ran alongside calling us names. I was amazed at this as I had been used to the friendly Indonesians back in Malang and I gazed at the floor with tears in my eyes. At Banyu Biru, we collected our belongings and jumped down from the truck onto the dusty road next to some very high walls that surrounded the infamous Banyu Biru prison. A large sign hung above the entrance confirming that it was in indeed the prison *'ROEMAH PENDJARA'* the Indonesian words for prison. When she saw the sign my poor mother almost fainted, 'Oh my God, oh my God, how terrible' she exclaimed. As we stumbled towards the prison gates and into a new nightmare, they were opened by a group of shabby looking Indonesian men. The look of shock and horror on their faces when they saw hundreds of haggard Dutch women and children approaching them has stayed with me ever since. Banyu Biru prison was a very old, dirty and dilapidated building and, as we were soon to find out, was a horrible place. It had originally been built by the Dutch to house around 1000 prisoners but now it was to become home for almost 5000 women and children. The prison camp commander was a Japanese Officer called Sakai, who, as we were later to discover, was a beast of a man. We were told that we must never look a Japanese guard in the eye and always to bow deeply to them. My mother and father had always taught me to look someone in the eye when they were talking to you and I found it really alien not to do this. I was well aware that however, that to do this would incur their wrath and result in a slap around the head or a kick on the shins. We were led down the labyrinth of corridors to ward fourteen and told that our mattresses would arrive shortly but, as we were all so tired from the journey, we just slumped down on the dirty floor and waited. I felt as though I had just arrived in hell.Eventually we were given four disgusting, dirty, foul smelling mattresses, not the clean ones that mother had packed the day before. At least we were able to put some clean sheets, which we had brought with us, over them. After the long journey we were all hungry and frightened. Once we were inside the Japanese locked the door to our ward, so we just lay down and huddled together for comfort. After what seemed like several hours the door was eventually opened and we were given some sort of a soup in a big barrel. There was just enough for a small bowl each but as we were so hungry we wolfed the lot down quickly. I seem to remember that it tasted good but, as I was so hungry anything would have tasted good to me on that terrible first day in that awful prison. As we were all crammed closely together, privacy was non existent as we lived cheek by jowel with the other inmates. As darkness fell over the prison we all settled down to try and get some much needed sleep. I had only just drifted off when I was awoken by the cries off pain from an elderly lady called Mrs Schaap. It had been obvious to us all she was unwell during the journey, and at around 5am the next morning she sadly passed away, the first person I was to see die in that terrible prison camp. There were to be many more deaths to follow over the coming months. Mrs Schaap's tragic death that night made a deep impression on Henny and I, one that was to stay with us for the rest of our lives. For the rest of the night I got little sleep as I was tormented by the hundreds of bed bugs that lived in the dirty mattresses. All four of us woke up badly bitten all over our bodies.

The next morning we were given a cup of weak tea (without sugar), along with a small bowl of a sort of starchy substance that I could hardly swallow. My mother forced me to eat it; she told me that I needed the nourishment to keep my strength up. This was to be our breakfast every morning for the duration of our stay in Banyu Biru prison camp. The Japanese told us that we must elect a leader for each ward and an overall leader for the whole prison camp. The camp leader would be held responsible for the behaviour of us all and the ward leader for those people living in her ward. Mrs. Eichelberg was elected our prison leader. We knuckled down to daily life and did our best to get on with our lives despite the filth and hardship. We tried our best to clean up our ward with the small amount of water and cleaning utensils we were given, but it was an almost impossible task. It was now nearing the end of February 1944 and although we did not know it at the time, this stinking prison was to be our home for the next twenty months. We were no longer known as internees but Prisoners of War, including even the youngest children and were all given a POW number that we had to keep throughout our internment. The Japanese told us that we had been put into prison camps to protect us from the Indonesians, an idea that was alien to me as I always considered the Indonesian people my friends.

One morning I awoke to the sound of shouting and screaming coming from outside the gates. When they were flung open another 950 women and children who had been transferred from Kediri and Madium in East Java, poured in. The prison was already crammed with over 4000 people, many more than it was designed for and to take in nearly another 950 was going to be almost impossible. Of course the Japanese were oblivious to our discomfort and had not the slightest sympathy for the many young children living in such dreadful circumstances. We were delighted to discover however, that Aunt Miep was among the newcomers and she was greeted with lots of hugs, kisses and tears. 'Your uncle Pierre is in the Kempetai prison in Batvia' she was able to tell us. Both the van Kampen brothers were now in Japanese internment camps.

Chapter 7

My First Job and Tenko

To keep us out of mischief, the Japanese ordered all children over the age of fourteen to work in the prison. I was given a job cutting the grass stalk by stalk with a small knife, not an onerous one but hard on the legs, boring and tiring. Ito, one of the Japanese guards, watched over us with a whip in his hand whilst we worked. We were not allowed to talk or to sit on the ground, only to squat on our haunches or kneel down. Initially we were only required to work three hours a day but as the weeks passed they increased it to four and then to five; it was then a long arduous day. The boys of around my age in the prison were required to work in the kitchen, a task for which they were delighted to receive extra food. They carried the tea barrels around the various wards each morning along with what I called, our 'starch breakfast', the same for lunch and again for the evening meal. They were also required to empty the 'poop-barrels', an extremely dirty job that required them to carry the heavy barrels and empty them into the sewers near to the toilets. Conditions in the wards were terrible and no matter how we tried we could not get rid of the bed bugs from our mattresses. We tried as best we could to clean them and then to hang then outside, but pesky little blighters kept coming back as we had no detergent or disinfectant to kill them off completely. With so many people living so close together arguments and quarrels broke out on a daily basis. As the younger children had nothing to do but hang around all day they frequently became bored and fought with each other. There was only one communal bathroom to each block where we all took showers in cold water. Women, children, boys and the girls all showered together. Initially we had some soap we had brought with us but as the months passed this ran out and we had to wash and shower with just water and our hands. My mother had brought a small washtub and some soap with her to wash our clothes, but that quickly ran out and we had to wash our clothes with salt and cold water. Consequently our clothes wore out quickly and we were reduced to wearing rags.

On the 10 June 1944 the Japanese decided that 400 women and children from our prison were to be transferred to Banyu Biru camp 11, a military complex nearby. We were not chosen to go but those who were, were happy to leave this dreadful prison with its oppressive high walls. The only consolation was that those of us who had to stay behind had a little more room. My mother asked if it would be possible for us to get a separate cell for the four of us and fortunately it was granted. We were able to leave the large crowded ward fourteen and move into a small cell. The only downside was that we had very little room to move around but at least we now had some privacy as a family. Lights out was strictly enforced at 10pm each evening on the orders of the Japanese prison camp Commander and we all went to bed together to sleep with our less than friendly bed bugs. In our new smaller cell, at least during the night we were able to leave the door ajar to get some fresh air. I yearned to get back to a normal life and away from this horrible place and often dreamt about being back in Sumber Sewu. I dreamt about walking in the jungle with my father, swimming in the pool and riding my horse Trip, but then I would awaken each morning to the reality of our tragic situation. After our tea and starch each morning we had to line up outside for *Kjotské* Japanese for *Tenko* (roll call). A Japanese guard would come along, shout *Kjotské* and we all had to stand up to attention as our names were shouted out. We had to confirm that we were present and if someone was ill and unable to attend the ward leader would inform the guard. This was ritual that was carried out all over the Far East under Japanese occupation and was universally detested. It usually lasted quite some time as the Japanese often got their counting wrong and they had to start all over again. Quite a few people collapsed in the strong sun and had to be helped back to their cell. When Tenko was completed he would shout *Kéré* and we all had to bow deeply towards Tokoyo to show our respect to the Japanese Emperor Hirohito. He would then shout *Nouré* (stand at ease) and we could relax again. Often he would make a speech to us but of course as it was in Japanese we didn't have clue what he was saying. It was always a relief when he shouted *Jasmé*, (dismiss) and we could go back to our cell. Food in the prison was the same every single day. Breakfast, as I mentioned earlier, was tea and a bowl of starch, lunch was a cup of boiled rice with a tablespoon of boiled green cabbage and a teaspoon of *sambal*, a sort of Spanish pepper. We would get a cup of tea again in the afternoon and dinner was a starch soup with a few leaves of cabbage. There were so few leaves that you could count them on one hand. My mother often said that it was just about enough to keep us alive – only just. As well as starvation the other major problem in the prison was disease, Malaria being the one we dreaded the most as mosquitoes were always a problem. I hated them. Just as you were about to fall asleep one would buzz around your head making sleep impossible. My mother, Jansje and I all succumbed to it over the months, but fortunately Henny did not catch it. She did, however, contact jaundice when her skin turned a terrible shade of yellow. Beri Beri was the most prevalent disease due to malnutrition. Fluid would accumulate, first in the feet and in the forearms, slowly progressing to the legs and upper arms before finally engulfing the whole body. The victim's heart would eventually fail and death followed immediately.

We had little in the way of medicines available to us and of course the lack of any fruit in our diet did not help either. There were three doctors in the prison, Dr. De Kock a surgeon from Surabaya, his wife who was a paediatrician and Dr. Kruine, and whilst they tried their best to keep everyone alive, they were helpless without a regular supply of medicines. The Japanese provided us with almost nothing.

Just before midnight on 31 August 1944, the Japanese guards ordered us out of bed for *Kjotské*. We had no idea why they did this but I had to stand for almost an hour with a tropical ulcer on the sole of my foot, it was agony. We had to listen to a long speech in Japanese in honour of Emperor Hirohito. It was translated into Dutch and we were told that we should be proud to stand erect in honour of his majesty the Emperor of Japan. It was quite ironic that this was also the birthday of our Queen Wilhelmina and of course all of my thoughts drifted back to my Dutch homeland and to our wonderful Queen. I suspect that the Japanese deliberately chose that date to insult us. When we were released, I stumbled back and collapsed onto my dirty mattress. My foot was still hurting terribly, due to standing on it for so long and I was unable to sleep. It was a long and painful night with my only solace thinking about our Queen.

The next morning I went to see Dr de Kock. 'I'm in a lot of agony with this ulcer Doctor, is there anything you can do for me?' I said to him. 'I can try and cut away the dead flesh for you Elizabeth' he replied. 'Let's have a look'. He proceeded to cut away the dead flesh with his famous razor blade, cleaned the ulcer, and bandaged my foot with some old bandages. Fortunately within a few days it had healed and I was able to walk properly again.

A couple of weeks later a group of boys all now over sixteen years old were transferred from our prison to Camp 8 in Ambarawa, not far from Banyu Biru. The Japanese had decided that all boys over the age of sixteen were to be separated from their mothers. Most were taken to men's prisons whilst some ended up in especially established boy's prisons. Once again this was extreme mental cruelty by the Japanese and many mothers suffered mental anguish at the loss of their sons. They fervently hoped that their sons might at least join their husbands in the men's prisons, but of course this was not guaranteed. When the war ended, some 3,600 Dutch boys in this age range had been interned away from their mothers and very often their fathers too. With the teenage boys away, the girls of my age now had to take-over the jobs they used to do. I now had to help plough the fields outside the camp and drag several old Dutch Cavalry loaded with all sorts of luggage to Ambarawa. It was very hard, physical work but I was happy to get out of the prison for a while, admire the beautiful panorama and see the real world again.

As the weeks went past more and more women and children began arriving into the prison. Six hundred arrived on the 19th of November from Karees and three days later 350 arrived from Tjihapit. With more mouths to feed we received less food and water, and of course there was less space and less privacy. The new arrivals always made the same comment when they arrived: 'What a horrible prison' Of course we were all too aware that it was a horrible prison. By now Sakai had been replaced as prison camp commander by Suzuki. We half expected him to come zooming into the camp on a motorcycle but he arrived one day sitting proudly in the back of a truck. Suzuki was also commander for camps 6, 7 and 9 in Ambarawa as well as camp 11 in Banyu Biru, so he had quite a big responsibility. He would appear now and then, give some orders, tell us what we had to do and then disappear to one of the other prisons.

As 1944 drew to a close the Japanese guards were gradually replaced by Koreans assisted by *Heihos*, (Indonesian volunteers in the Japanese Army). More than 40,000 Indonesians were now serving in the Japanese army and they, along with the Koreans, had little experience of running POW camps. They had usually only completed a crash course on guarding prisoners of war, a course that did not teach them much more than anti-Allied propaganda. The new guards were primitive ill educated men, who generally lacked any knowledge of the customs of the European prisoners and of course we knew little about Japanese customs and practices. Naturally this often led to a lack of mutual understanding between prisoners and guards. As the fortunes of war were now turning against the Japanese, they began organizing the Indonesians into military and paramilitary units. Many Indonesians saw the Japanese occupation as a way of getting their independence from Holland and were happy to join them in a war that they thought would bring them independence. Whilst walking into Ambarawa one day we passed some Indonesians hanging around on the side of the road. Normally the local people would shout to us or give us a wave but, on that day they just looked the other way. It was probably because we had a Japanese guard with us and they were just as scared of the Japanese as we were. Of course most of them felt sorry for us as we must have looked terrible, compared to the healthy people they worked with before the invasion. We were thin, emaciated, walking barefoot and dressed in rags. Christmas was only a few days away when on our walk into Ambarawa, we met some Dutch people from Banyu Biru camp 11. Our group leader managed to exchange a few words with one of them who told her that someone in their prison had a small radio. 'Over the airwaves we heard that the Japanese are losing the war and that the Americans are closing in on Tokoyo' she whispered. When we got back to the prison I told my mother this exciting news but she refused to believe me: 'Don't listen to rumours Elizabeth, they are rarely true' she said. Of course this really deflated me as I was so excited that perhaps the end of our internment was in sight. Not a day passed when I did not think about my father incarcerated in the Kempeitai prison. With Christmas just round the corner I knew that he would also be very hungry and would be thinking about a Christmas without his wife and his three daughters. It was heart wrenching and tears trickled down my cheeks. Christmas day 1944 duly arrived and to us it was just another day in this dreary cheerless prison. We tried to celebrate as best we could but most people simply wanted the whole bad dream to end and to get back to their loved ones. We had been interned now for seven months but it seemed more like seven years.

As 1945 dawned, again we had little to celebrate. The only Happy New Year greetings we passed amongst ourselves were to hope that 1945 would really be a happy year for us all. I was getting malaria attacks every few weeks and to carry on working was very hard when you had malaria, but nonetheless I had to go out to work every day. As well as the malaria attacks I constantly had head lice. They were rife throughout the prison and even though I washed my hair every day with just cold water I could not get rid of them. Without any sort of shampoo or chemicals it was just impossible to get rid of the little beggars. We were always on the look out for plants that we could eat to supplement our meagre diet. One day whilst I was outside working on the land, a Heiho told us that there was some wild purslane near to where we were working. Although considered a weed in many countries, purslane can be eaten as a leaf vegetable as its soft succulent leaves contain omega-3 fatty acids. It has a slightly sour and salty taste, the stem, leaves and flower buds are all edible and it can be used fresh as a salad or stir-fried. It can also be added to or can be used in soups and stews. We all stuffed a bunch of the plant under our clothes and took it back to the prison, where my mother washed it and mixed it in with our cabbage starch soup for dinner. It was a welcome addition to our meagre diet. We also found some edible snails which we boiled in water several times over and then mixed them into our rice - they tasted delicious. We were by now seriously malnourished and many people were suffering from tropical ulcers that were very difficult to get rid off. The most abiding memory for me was the smell, as with so many people living in close proximity and with no soap or detergent, we all stank to high heaven. For some reason the Japanese did not allow any music to be played or listened to in the prison. I always loved to listen to music and for two years of my life I was deprived of that wonderful experience, thank you Japanese captors. The Japanese guards now became very agitated and angry over very small issues, yelling at us constantly and often slapping our faces for no reason at all. Although we did not know it at the time this was probably because the war was now starting to swing against them. It seemed as though they were actually enjoying the pain, suffering and discomfort that they were inflicting on us. They were treating women and children like starving rats. I often wonder if they had been getting some sort of 'high' out of treating us like animals. From waking up in the morning until going to sleep at night all I could think off was food. Mother started writing recipes on every single piece of paper she could find and when I came back from work she would read them out aloud to me, whilst I salivated at the thoughts. I have no idea why she did this and looking back now it seemed cruel. Anyone over fifteen years of age was required to do a two hour duty every fortnight. I was allocated the two to four am shift. It was a terrible time, I just had to sit in the darkness with an empty stomach waiting for the sun to rise - I hated it. Quite why we had to do it and what this achieved I do not know. We worked in pairs walking around our section of the camp on the lookout for smugglers. Naturally we did the opposite and warned the smugglers when the Japanese guards were around. Mothers would part with anything they had of value to try and buy food for their children and often took incredible risks to trade things with the native Indonesians in order to keep their skeletal children from dying. The Indonesians themselves took great risks as they were often punished even more harshly for bartering with us. When we passed a guard he would ask us *'Donata deska?'* (Have you seen any smugglers).We had to bow deep and answer; **'***Fu simban itju ari masin'***.** He would ask us in a bit of English and a bit of Malay (today Bahasa Indonesia) if we had seen any smugglers. We answered 'No' we hadn't seen anybody at all. When the Japanese soldier left us we had to bow again and say; '*Su swi teh fuku musi mah*'. We had to learn these Japanese words but I still have no idea what they really mean. Maybe we had to say something like 'I am the night-watcher and everything is okay.' Who knows? I wrote those Japanese words down just in case I might forget them; if I had I would have been slapped in the face. It was quite cold during the night, our worn-out clothes gave us little warmth and we did not even get a drink of tea or coffee during our shift. It was pitch black during the night as the Japanese insisted that all lights were turned off in case 'the enemy' flew over and identified our prison camp.

One very dark cold night whilst I was on patrol I heard several women crying out in pain. I crept round the corner of a block and saw two women being beaten by a guard with a split bamboo stick. The Japanese soldiers were always using split bamboos as it would leave splinters in the skin. I recognised Mrs to-Water and Mrs Damen as the two who were getting beaten and I almost cried with pity for them. As I was a bit older now, I was given a job loading *barang-barang* (goods) onto the military cavalry carts and taking them to Ambarawa. I always really enjoyed the walk into the town with my working group, even though it was a long walk barefoot on the hot asphalt road. At Ambarawa we arrived into another world, one that I remembered very well before the invasion. The smell of the food being cooked on the stalls outside the railway station was tantalising, I yearned to buy some but of course we did not have any money to do so. It was amazing how normal life went on outside of our dirty prison; it was as though this was a different world. I loved the sights and smells around the station and could have stood for hours just starting at the locomotives. People were arriving and departing all the time and they must have been surprised when they saw the condition we were in. Before we set off on the return journey we were given a small piece of not risen bread. It tasted delicious to a half starved teenager but I would always tuck half of it away to take back to my mother and my sisters. After we had loaded the military cavalry carts again we had to set off for the walk back to the prison, a journey that was always much harder than the journey out. I felt so sad returning to that stinking prison but at least I knew that I had my mother and sisters to go back to. It would have been wonderful to simply jump onto one of the trains and go back to our lovely home but I knew that that was unlikely to happen.

Chapter 8

Goodbye to the little Boys

On 16 January 1945, the Japanese took sixty-five little boys out of the prison and away from their mothers. The boys, all around nine or ten years of age, were transported to camp 7 in nearby Ambarawa, a prison for boys and old men. I can still see the looks of terror on the faces of those little boys as, with their little bit of luggage, they were loaded onto trucks and driven out of the gates. It is a memory that will live with me forever. The boys had already been separated from their fathers and now they were taken away from their mothers -for what reason? How could the Japanese be so cruel? The mothers of the little boys had already lost their husbands, many of whom were scattered all over SE Asia, now their sons had also been taken away from them. They were all simply distraught with grief. Would their children be taken care off? Would they be fed? Would they be mistreated? The whole prison went into mourning. As we were three girls we were able to stay with our mother and we gave thanks for that. Several of the women who had their sons taken away from them, had mental breakdowns. One woman thought that someone in the prison was hiding her son so she spent days looking all over for him. I often wondered if these women were all reunited with their sons after the war.

One night whilst on duty I heard someone screaming. A naked woman came running round a corner heading for the Japanese quarters. One of the guards grabbed her, bundled her into a car and drove her out of the camp never to be seen again. Some time later we heard that she had died, but how she died we shall never know.

The Japanese guards would often summon us to gather round to listen to a speech as to how well they were doing and that the war would be won soon. One day we were all summoned to gather around a guard. He stood arrogantly with his interpreter, a Swedish national who spoke Dutch and Japanese, alongside him. 'Who has been smuggling?' he shouted. 'If you do not own up then the whole camp will be punished', he added. There was silence and no one owned up. Many of the women became very angry. 'If you have been smuggling, own up otherwise the children will all suffer', they shouted. Still no one came forward and the Japanese guard became really angry. 'Then the whole camp shall be punished and you shall have no water until tomorrow morning,' he said. Mother and the rest of the women were furious but there was nothing they could do as they had no idea who had been smuggling. For the next twelve hours we were deprived of even a small glass of water. The guards became extra vigilant and a few days' later two women and a young girl were caught smuggling. The whole ward was summoned to appear before the guards. 'These women will be hanged tomorrow and you will all gather to watch', a guard announced. At noon the next day, the three women were marched out with their hands tied behind their backs. They were then tied to bamboo poles with their toes just touching the ground and left hanging there in the blazing sun for the rest of the day without food or water. 'We have decided to spare them their lives but anyone else caught smuggling will be executed' a guard shouted. As soon as the sun went down we rushed out, cut them down and carried them back to their cells. They were completely exhausted and dehydrated. Punishments like this were handed out for even the slightest misdemeanours. One day when we were returning from work outside the prison we saw some large black cars parked just outside the gates. As we entered we were ordered to join a line of teenage girls and young women lined up in front of several Japanese Officers. The Officers marched down the line eyeing us for head to toe. As I was still suffering from an attack of Malaria I was trembling and there was only one thought in my mind 'please let me lie down and rest'. As the Officers passed me I kept my head down and didn't dare to look up, fortunately I was not picked out. Most of the young women were crying as they were led away. I heard later that they were taken to Japanese camps to act as 'comfort women' for the troops. Many mothers had shaved the heads of their daughters and dressed them as boys to try and avoid them being taken away. Some others volunteered themselves to save their daughters and others simply volunteered hoping for a better access to food and conditions, whilst others did it to protect younger more vulnerable women. When we were dismissed I ran in tears to my mother and sisters. They were very upset and had been so scared that the Japanese would take me away. Several of the young women who had been taken away that day left behind children who had to be looked after by other mothers in the prison. It was such a sad day for all of us.

At the end of the war between two and three hundred Dutch women were working, either by force or voluntarily, in Japanese 'comfort stations'. The Dutch Government sought justice for these women and a court martial in Batvia in February 1948 tried thirteen Japanese military leaders. One was sentenced to death for the forced prostitution of Dutch women whilst eleven others were given prison sentences. Very few of the survivors spoke about their experiences as comfort women, but fifty years later Jos Hagers a female correspondent for de Telegraaf in Amsterdam wrote a newspaper article about the wartime forced prostitution of Dutch women in the East Indies. Hagers, now a top correspondent and investigative reporter for De Telegraaf, was born in an internment camp in Sumatra, and spent the first three and a half years of her life crammed with 51,500 other children and their mothers in a former Catholic girls' school meant to hold 5,000 students.

By March 194, Banyu Biru prison had over 4,500 women and children languishing within its walls. For some reason, over the next few weeks many male prisoners started to arrive adding to an already overcrowded camp. Of course as each day passed we hoped that our father might be amongst them, and each morning we jumped out of bed waiting for more new arrivals. But it was not to be. It was now clear to everyone that the Japanese were now losing the war, but many women and children were still dying of starvation in that dreadful prison. Life was really hard for the women and children in the camp. My youngest sister Jansje became very quiet and withdrawn, just sitting staring into space for most of the day. I got a very bad malaria attack and Doctor De Kock was worried that I might die as my temperature was dangerously high. I can recall lying on my mattress as my mind floated up into the clouds as though I was flying on a magic carpet. I could hear Doctor De Kock saying to my mother; 'I hope that Elizabeth will stay alive, I am extremely worried, I have hardly any quinine left but I'll give her some tablets'. Fortunately the quinine helped to reduce my temperature and that terrible malaria attack passed in a few days. When I woke up every morning my first thoughts were of my father. Where was he? Is he ill? Is he hungry? Is he still in Malang? What was happening to him? I felt sure that he was still alive. I don't know why, but I just did. We were all well aware of the way the Japanese treated their prisoners but we hoped that he was no longer in a Kempeitai prison Perhaps he was now in a camp for men in Malang or elsewhere or that he might even be in a camp not too far away from Banyu Biru 10. I never stopped thinking about my father as I missed him so much.

On 3 May, 600 women and children were transferred to our prison from Ambarawa camp 9, and four weeks later 500 women and children came in from the Solo camp. It was now extremely crowded as there were now around 5,300 women and children desperately trying to stay alive in this filthy, smelly hell hole. As well as bouts of malaria I had now contracted beri-beri through a lack of vitamins, and my face and stomach were badly swollen. Mother had begun to lose some of her teeth and she had constant toothache. Some of the women in the camp resorted to stealing eggshells from the Japanese dustbins and put them on fires to grind down to make a source of calcium. We really had to fight hard to just stay alive, taking one day at a time.

It was now mid-August 1945 and one Sunday morning we heard an aeroplane flying overhead. Rushing out to have a look, we were delighted to see the red white and blue of the Dutch flag on the fuselage and tailplane. It seemed strange though that there was no shooting from the Japanese anti-aircraft guns. We all waved madly up at the pilot as he flew over. 'Is the war over' we all shouted at the tops of our voices in the vain hope that the pilot would hear us. Suddenly it began to snow, as hundreds of leaflets came falling down from the sky, covering the camp like confetti at a wedding. Everyone started running around picking them up and I took one straight back to my mother. She smiled broadly when she read it. 'The war is over girls, we will be free soon' she said excitedly. The leaflet was signed by the commander of the Dutch East Indies Army, General L.H. van Oyen who was now based in Canberra. It told us that the war was almost over and we would soon be released. We all hugged each other; this was the most beautiful Sunday we had all experienced in three years and we knelt down and thanked God. Our euphoria was to be short lived as a few minutes later a car came screeching through the gates. Several Japanese officers jumped out and started screaming at us; they were absolutely furious because now we all knew that Japan was losing the war. We were ordered to line up to be addressed by the prison commander. 'You must all hand over the leaflets that you have found' he shouted. 'Anyone who tries to hide one will be severely punished and you will all go without food for the rest of the day'. 'You must destroy that leaflet Elizabeth' mother whispered. 'But mother I want to keep it as a souvenir' I said. She became very angry with me and I saw that she was really very scared so I began to tear up the leaflet into small pieces. I dropped the tiny shreds all over the camp as I walked back to our cell. I wish now that I had had the courage to hide the leaflet away, it would have been a wonderful souvenir.

Although we were now all in high spirits with the news that the end of the war was in sight, life in the prison actually got worse. There was always this eternal gnawing hunger and the hope for better days started fading away again. Was the news really true? Mothers were still desperate for food for their children as many stopped growing due to lack of vitamins and indeed many died in their mother's arms just a matter of weeks before the end of the war. It was so sad that children were dying on a daily basis with the war just about over.

On the 23rd August, something strange happened. We were given a little bit more food than usual and it also seemed to be of a better quality. The Japanese guards were very quiet and left us alone for most of the day, something was definitely happening. As we prepared to go out to work that day we were told that we would no longer have to leave the prison and go to work.

Chapter 9

Freedom at last and Farewell Indonesia

It was on the 24 August 1945 when Mrs. Eichelberg our prison leader asked us all to gather outside where she was stood next to a very serious looking commandant. 'Ladies, the war is over, you are now all free women, Japan surrendered to the Allies nine days ago on 15 August and for some reason our guards have kept it to themselves', she said in a faltering voice. For several seconds there was a stunned silence before we took in the magnitude of what she had said and then we all clapped, cheered and hugged each other, we were free. A small group of women started singing the Dutch anthem De Wilhelmus and of course we all joined in. It was so uplifting to once again be singing our national anthem after two years of hell in this dirty, smelly prison. More than 160 women and children had died in the Banyu Biru prison during those terrible two years. When someone died they were simply laid on a bamboo stretcher and carried outside the prison to be buried not too far away. With our ordeal finally over my thoughts once again now turned to my father. Surely he would soon come to find us now and we would be reunited as a loving family again. My sister Jansje was now eight and she was delighted that we were free and that we were given more food. As we were now free, the next day I decided to walk to Fort Willem camp where I knew that there were some men who came from Malang and who might know my father. As I approached the camp, I asked the first man I met if he knew Theo van Kampen. 'He is not here but if I find out anything about him I will come to your camp and let you know', he said helpfully.

Back in the prison Mrs Eichelberg told us that is was now no longer advisable to go out. 'With the war over, many of the Indonesians are seizing the opportunity to free themselves from Dutch rule and several Dutch people had been murdered' she told us.

This uprising was called the *Bersiap'*(meaning to be ready). Ironically, the Japanese who had made our life a misery over the previous two years, were now protecting us from these angry young Indonesians and it felt very strange to be liberated but not yet completely free. We were to learn later that many ex-war prisoners had been killed by Indonesian *permuda*s (young rebels) in the weeks and months just after the war ended. Over one hundred Dutch women and children were murdered by the *permuda* as they tried to leave their camp in Surabaya. The large majority of the Dutch in and outside the Dutch East Indies did not realise that the situation in the colony had changed drastically as a result of the war. We all blindly assumed that Dutch colonial rule would be restored and did not take the independence movement seriously.

On 17 August, just a matter of days after the end of the war, Sukarno who had been head of the puppet administration during Japanese rule proclaimed Indonesia a Republic. The Japanese had been impressed by Sukarno's following in Indonesia and he had been a valuable asset to them with their need to mobilise the indigenous population for the war effort. When the Japanese occupied Indonesia in 1942, Sukarno had been languishing in jail and of course when they promised to release him if he and his followers agreed to co-operate with them, he readily agreed. He knew that it would be his best chance of gaining independence from the Dutch. When the war ended, Sukarno's reputation became tarnished due to his role in recruiting between four and ten million *romusha* (forced labourers), who had suffered an 80% death rate during the Japanese occupation. Prior to the Japanese invasion nationalists of The Dutch East Indies were already demanding freedom from Dutch rule and of course the Japanese were well aware of this. They used it to advance their aims by promising the Indonesian people freedom to run their own affairs.

With war over and the Japanese defeated, the Dutch Government sent a new civil administration that had been held in readiness in Australia out to Java. The vast majority of us did not realise that the situation both inside and outside the colony had now changed dramatically as a result of the war. We assumed that colonial rule would continue as before and we did not take the Declaration of Independence by the Indonesians seriously. For the four years following the Japanese capitulation the Indonesian rebels led by Sukarno were to fight a bloody war against Dutch rule. On 13 October, the IPA (Indonesian Peoples Army) declared war on the Dutch, Eurasians and Ambonese and two weeks later the battle of Surabaya broke out with more than five thousand Dutch Nationals losing their lives during this period of bitter fighting. Back in Holland the Government refused to bow to force but indicated that it was ready to 'deliberate' as they put it, with the Indonesians. This offer did not satisfy the nationalists who insisted on nothing less than complete independence. Life in the prison was considerably better now; we were given more food and our Japanese guards were a lot friendlier towards us.

One morning Henny and I saw one of the Japanese guards crying; apparently the atomic bomb had killed his whole family back in Hiroshima. We did actually feel a tinge of sadness for him. The task of liberating and protecting us from the threat of militant nationalists was delegated to the British forces led by General Christison, with the first troops arriving on 29 September. A few days later the Japanese guards simply vanished and a regiment of British Ghurkhas entered the camp. We were delighted to be under the control of the British forces and the quality and amount of food now increased even more. It was to prove a difficult task for the Ghurkhas as they had to simultaneously disarm the Japanese, protect us and keep the Indonesian militants at bay. There was little adequate transportation, little medical help and not enough men to manage such an enormous task, so we had to sit tight and wait. Meanwhile the Japanese wanted to get rid of their responsibilities for maintaining order and started to withdraw into camps that that had already prepared for such an eventuality. The British did however keep many Japanese in charge of camps and general administration as they were not yet in a position to take over. The repatriation of British Prisoners of War naturally took priority. Many of the Japanese troops handed over their weapons to Indonesian youth groups, making the situation worse. The country was in chaos. British aircraft flew over and dropped crates containing corned beef, biscuits, chocolates, cigarettes, milk powder, sugar, coffee, soap and much more. It was heaven for us compared to what we had been used to over the past two years and as an added bonus we collected the parachute material to made clothes. My mother made me a beautiful blouse out of a parachute. We started cleaning up the *gudangs* (stores) and were shocked to discover boxes full of medicines such as anti-malaria tablets, quinine and many others. If the Japanese had issued these to us during our imprisonment, the lives of many women and children who died in this prison might have been saved. There were also many letters and cards addressed to people in the prison that had never been delivered. We all felt very sad and angry that they had deprived us of even basic contact with our families.

We were advised by the British to remain in the prison until such time as they deemed it safe for us to leave. We were told that they had evacuation plans in place and very soon we would all be moved out. Some families disregarded this advice and left to try and find their way home but mother decided that we should stay until father was able to join us.

Day by day more and more men entered the prison to join their wives and children and each day we hoped that our father would walk through the gates, but he never arrived. We just had no news at all of his whereabouts. We fervently hoped that one day he would walk through the gates or that we would receive a letter from him. Just before we were scheduled to leave mother fell ill. She had bad diarrhoea, couldn't stop vomiting and her temperature rocketed. Our neighbours thought it might be typhoid so they stayed away as they thought it was contagious. As all the Doctors had now left the prison we had to take care of her ourselves, giving her boiled water to drink and feeding her boiled rice. We were terrified that we might lose our mother just as we were about to be released, but fortunately after about a week she began to recover and soon was completely well again.

On 3 October, Dr van Mook, Lt. Governor General of the Dutch East Indies arrived in Batvia from Australia accompanied by Admiral Helfrich, C in C of the Dutch forces in the East along with some Dutch troops. Extreme elements of the Nationalists tried to prevent the Dutch troops from landing and were disrupting the British efforts to rescue POWs. In central Java the Indonesians started rounding up Dutch citizens who had left the safety of the camps and throwing them into prisons. Many people were beaten and others hacked to pieces by Indonesian freedom fighters out of control. Sukarno and the other nationalist leaders were unable to fully control their young and excitable followers. Many combat groups were formed using Japanese weapons that had been taken. Batvia was placed under Allied Military administration on 27 October and a military government was set up in Surabaya. To his credit Soekarna disapproved of military force by the extremists and commenced negotiations with the van Mook government at the beginning November. The negotiations quickly broke down and on 13 November Dr Sjhrir took over as leader of the nationalists from Soekarno and agreed to submit the question of nationalism to the UN Council. He distanced himself from the extremists who were still trying to hamper the British in their rescue mission.

It was a full two months after the Japanese surrendered before we eventually left that hell hole of a prison camp. We were one of the last groups to leave and it was a wonderful feeling to at last walk out into the fresh air and freedom after two years of internment. The wonderful Ghurkha soldiers helped us up into open trucks on which they had placed mattresses to try and make our journey a bit more comfortable. We didn't know where they were taking us, but we didn't care as we trusted them implicitly and were going home; that was all that mattered. After about a two hour drive we arrived at a camp called 'Halmaheira', near Semarang. This camp was like paradise compared to Banyu Biru 10; it had clean modern toilets instead of holes in the floor, breakfast was wonderful and there were lovely doctors and nurses to attend to all our needs. I felt as though I had just been transported from hell into heaven. As my hair was still full of lice the nurses washed it with modern shampoo and the lice soon disappeared. Our clothes were washed with wonderful smelling washing powder and I shall never forget that first piece of Palmolive soap that I was given. It was such a luxury to have a bath again for the first time in over two years. Our nightmare was over at last but we now had to begin the process of trying to rebuild our shattered lives. We had left that nightmare in a dirty smelly prison far behind us for ever, but little did I know then that another nightmare was about to begin. As I lay on that beautiful mattress that first night, my thoughts again were of my father, as they had done every night for the past two years - I just had to find him.

The next day mother and I went down to the nearest police office to try and find out if anyone knew about the whereabouts of my father. The officers there were very friendly and helpful and telephoned around all the police offices in the area. Unfortunately no-one knew anything about a Theo van Kampen. 'We will find your husband, Mrs van Kampen, I will telephone you at your camp as soon as we find out anything', promised the Chief of Police, but of course mother and I were still in despair and both very distraught.

Almost three months had now passed since the Japanese surrender and just before Christmas 1945 we were told that we were to be evacuated back to Holland. We had still heard nothing at all about the whereabouts of our father and we did not want to go and leave him behind. We were given no choice however, as it was becoming too dangerous to remain in Indonesia and we had no means of supporting ourselves. A few days before we were due to leave, mother received a letter from aunt Miep informing us that uncle Pierre had died a year earlier in a Kempeitai prison in Jakarta. Naturally we were all devastated to get this tragic news as we loved our uncle Pierre dearly. Of course this made us worry even more about father.

It was on 28 December 1945 when, along with 349 other Dutch evacuees, we were transported to the HMS *Princess Beatrix* a commando troop ship of the British Royal navy, waiting in Semarang harbour. Originally built as a civilian passenger liner in 1939 at Vlissingen in the Netherlands, the *Beatrix* fled to Britain after the German invasion and was taken over by the Royal Navy. A flotilla of small boats took us out to the ship where we were made most welcome by the British crew. Hammocks had been strung up in the hold and I had to help little Jansje as she was too little to climb onto the hammock herself. After we had settled into our berths, the huge engines started up and we all quickly made our way up to the deck to wave farewell to Indonesia, a country that we all loved. I felt completely empty. We were leaving our father behind in Java and nothing seemed to matter anymore as I just stared at all the people on the quayside busy working, talking and laughing. With Commander Benjamin Evans DSC, RNR in charge, slowly the *Princess Beatrix* crept out of the harbour en route to Ceylon and from there back to Holland. As the coast of Java disappeared behind us and with the wind blowing my hair in all directions, my thoughts were again of my father and how he would have loved to have been with us. Tears rolled down my cheeks. As the coast of Java slowly sunk beneath the horizon, I shouted 'Farewell beautiful Indonesia'.

On board the *Beatrix*, the British Navy looked after us well. The crew organized games for the children and it was wonderful to once again laugh and play without worrying about being shouted at or beaten. It was just like going on a holiday. The ship's first port of call was Colombo, the capital of Ceylon (now Sri Lanka), where we were taken by train to an ex British military camp in Kandy, a small town fifty miles away up in the mountains. In the camp we were allocated a large room with four camp beds. The dining room served delicious meals, especially the curries and the full English breakfast of bacon, eggs and toast with lots of cups of tea. It was just heaven to be free and eat this wonderful food. There were also several Dutch teachers making their way home and they decided to start classes for the children. It had been four long years without education for most of the children on board and we were all delighted to get back to our studies. At first I found it difficult to adjust to reading books again, but in that camp in Ceylon I set about my studies as I knew how important it was to try and catch up. Life in Kandy camp was wonderful but unfortunately three of the van Kampen family were again struck down with illness while we were there. Henny had to spend some time in the military hospital as she was still suffering from jaundice. Jansje also had to be taken to the hospital as she had developed measles, and to make matters worse, our mother became paralysed on the left side of her face and body. She too was taken to the hospital and I felt really lonely. Fortunately they all quickly recovered and we were all together again as a family after a few weeks.

Chapter 10

Father is Dead

My father Theo van Kampen

It was now the end of January 1946 and mother received a letter from aunt Miep, who had travelled back to Holland some weeks earlier. How she knew how to contact us in Ceylon I just don't know. She wrote to say that she had found my father's name on a list of

Dutch nationals who had died in the Dutch East Indies before the Japanese capitulation. We were all heartbroken and hugged each other, but were still optimistic that it was a mistake and he was still alive. We simply refused to believe that he was dead; perhaps his name had been confused with someone else? 'We will live in hope that this is a mistake girls

Due to our mother's illness we had to remain in the camp and were unable to board the *Beatrix* for its journey back to Holland. Towards the end of February the slender hopes that our father was still alive were dashed when we got a letter from the Red Cross in Batavia informing us that according to Japanese statements they had regarding deceased prisoners; 'Theo van Kampen died in Malang prison of *Cachexie,* (dehydration)'. It read. What it actually meant was that my father had been murdered by the Kempetai. It felt as though someone had stabbed me in the heart.

We stayed in the camp in Ceylon for over four months before mother was well enough for us to be able to set off for Holland. On 15 May, along with 1100 other Dutch nationals we boarded the SS *Kota Baroe* in Colombo, bound for Rotterdam. With so many people on board the crew asked if any of us would like a job. I immediately volunteered and got my first ever job serving meals to the other passengers. I was paid 100 guilders that I gave to my mother, a sum that felt like a fortune to us at the time. I really enjoyed the work and met lots of people on the journey back to Holland. Our first stop was at Suez, where on docking we transported the ten miles or so by train to Ataqa. As we were heading for a much cooler climate we were all given some warm clothes as our existing clothes were only suitable for the tropics. Mother was given a set of white and orange pyjamas, and when she tried them on she looked like a clown. We all couldn't stop laughing but at least they were in the Dutch colours.

The next morning we were transported back to the ship to begin our voyage through the Suez Canal. The trip through the 109 miles of the canal was amazing and when we docked at Port Said, all sorts of little boats surrounded the ship. The local people streamed on board selling all sorts of colourful goods. My mother bought a very nice handbag.

It was 11 June when we eventually arrived home into the port of Rotterdam, almost one month since we left Ceylon. The captain played the Dutch national anthem over the ship's speakers as we walked down the gangplank onto Dutch soil again for the first time in ten years. On board the ship we had already been asked where we wanted to be taken when we got back to Holland. Mother told them that we wanted to be taken either to The Hague where her parents lived, or to Helmond where our aunt was living in our grandparent's house. For some reason we were taken to neither but were bussed fifty miles to Wijk aan Zee, a small village near the sea, not too far from Haarlem.

In Wijk aan Zee we were shown to a room in a guest house that was already full with many other people who had been repatriated from the Dutch East Indies.

We were all very excited to be back in Holland and the next morning mother wrote letters to our grandparents and to Aunt Marie in Helmond. She asked me if I would pop out to the post office and post the two letters. It was quite strange walking to the post office as it was the first time I had been out on my own in Holland. Several people spoke to me and as they seemed to be aware that I was refugee from the Dutch East Indies, many of them were quite abusive towards me and called me 'the daughter of a nasty exploiter, a slave driver, from the Dutch East Indies'. After six years of oppressive Nazi, they thought that we had had an easy ride during the war and were bitter towards us. In Holland at that time, Dutch colonial citizens were portrayed in a very negative way and many people thought that we had exploited the Indonesian population. Of course I knew that this was far from the case and kept very quiet, but I was deeply hurt by the abuse I received from my fellow Dutch citizens in those early days.

Mother quickly set about trying to find accommodation for the four of us. A few days later she found a house that we could afford to rent in Haarlem and as she got a small pension based on my father's previous employment in Holland, we were able to be self-sufficient. She also found a nice school for Henny and Jansje. The house in Haarlem felt really cold as we had been used to living in a tropical climate. At night when we went to bed we would put newspapers on top of our blankets to keep warm and each morning we had to boil ice cold water in order to have a wash. Once a week we went to a communal bath house to take a shower, life back in the Netherlands was so very different from what I was used to in Indonesia. In Indonesia before the Japanese invasion, I was at the end of the first class of the MULO, an advanced elementary education. In Haarlem I was put into the second class of the HBS (former Dutch High school) and because of what I had gone through I really struggled with my classes. Of course none of the teachers listened as they thought I was just lazy and at the end of that school year I failed my exams. I really struggled with German and as all the rest of the girls in my class could already speak the language due to the German occupation of the country, I was left behind.

Chapter 11

A Career, a Husband and Travel

I left school in July 1947 and obtained a job working for a bank in Amsterdam. It took me fifteen minutes by train each day to get into the city and I really enjoyed meeting new people. I found the job quite boring, but whilst working at the bank at least I was able to further my education by studying bookkeeping in the evenings. It was a trend at that time to have pen friends and I wrote lots of letters in English to pen friends all over the world. Ironically one was a Japanese boy from Tokyo. We wrote to each other over several years and he sent me lots of nice postcards with views of the city.

The Dutch people I met in Amsterdam told me many stories about the horrors of the German occupation of Holland but I was reluctant to discuss the Japanese occupation of the Dutch East Indies. I never talked about my father as the memories were just so depressing. One of my pen-friends at that time was Eileen, an English girl from Nottingham. Eileen came over to stay with us for ten days in the summer of 1948 and we struck up an instant friendship.
'Can you find me a job in England Eileen?' I said as she was leaving to go home. 'I'll do my best Elizabeth, perhaps we can get you a job as an au pair she said.
A couple of months later she wrote to me to tell me that she had got me an offer of a job as an au pair for a family with three children in Nottingham. I immediately said yes, and in October 1948 I set off for England to begin a new phase in my life.

Located in the North Midlands on the river Trent, I found Nottingham a very friendly city. The family I worked for were very nice but after six months I was really missing my family and wanted to go back to Holland.
A month or so later I waved Eileen goodbye and caught a flight back to Amsterdam, where I applied to be a student nurse. My

application was immediately accepted as there was a shortage of nurses in Holland at that time.

On starting my nursing course I was shocked to find myself in the kitchens washing the dishes for the first month; it would appear that as I was from the Dutch East Indies I had to do this to practice using my hands. I made very good friends during my time as a student nurse and was delighted when a group of us discovered a small Indonesian café not far from Amsterdam Central Station. We would visit the café a couple of times a week and listen to an Indonesian group singing songs from their homeland. When I closed my eyes I felt as though I was back in Malang and I dreamt of becoming a nurse in Indonesia, perhaps even in Malang.

My nursing training was most enjoyable and the first year just flew past. Several weeks into my second year however, I developed a stomach ulcer and was confined to bed for six weeks ands put on a special diet. Naturally my training suffered badly as studying was difficult and I struggled to keep up with the work. After several weeks laid up in hospital they reluctantly informed me that they would have to terminate my course. This was a hammer blow to me as I had put so much time and effort into the first year, but I was made of stern stuff and vowed to get on with my life. As a Prisoner of War I was used to putting difficult circumstances behind me so I accepted my fate and looked forward to the next phase of my life.

What should I do next? I still had a bit of wanderlust in me and when one of my friends told me that she knew a French family in Lyon France who were looking for an au pair to look after their three children during the summer holidays, I jumped at the chance. She gave me their address and I wrote to them applying for the job. They accepted immediately and a week later I was on my way to France.

I spent three months with the French family and it was a glorious time. I just loved the French culture and acquired a taste for French food and French wine, but as the job was only for one summer I returned home to Haarlam and my family.

In January 1951, I met Richard who was later to become my husband and on 28 August 1952 we were married in Amstelveen a small town close to Amsterdam. For the next four years we worked hard to save money as we both had a desire to emigrate.

In 1956, all former inmates of POW camps in the former Dutch East Indies were given a payment of two hundred and seventy five Guilders from the Dutch Government as compensation for their hardships in the camps. The money was very welcome and helped with our plans for the future. I wanted to go and live in Canada but Richard wanted to go to the *USA,* but as it happened we went to neither. Richard's brother had emigrated to South Africa the previous year and had written to him telling him how wonderful the country was and on that basis we decided to go to South Africa. It was a wrench to once again leave my mother and two sisters behind in Holland, but as I really wanted to start a new life with Richard I just had to go. Before we left, mother said to me 'I always knew that you would be a globetrotter Elizabeth, so good luck'.

When we had our passports in order we set off from Amsterdam for Johannesburg via Cape Town on board the Waterman. The Waterman's crew were mainly Indonesian, and it was nice to be able to talk with them about their country and especially Malang, my spiritual home.

After spending a few days in Cape Town we took the train to Johannesburg. It was a very long and hot journey through the Great Karroo desert and when we finally arrived we were both exhausted. We rented an apartment in a quarter of Johannesburg called Hillbrow and started looking for jobs. A week later Richard got a job working for Philips, a Dutch company, and I got one working for a British Company, Barclays Bank as a bookkeeping-machine-operator.

My father was still always in my mind and I decided to write a letter to the prison governor of the Lowok Waru ex-Kempeitai prison in Malang asking about my father's grave. To his credit he responded immediately and informed me that there was no known grave in the name Theo van Kampen. I was so disappointed.

Richard and I lived and worked in Johannesburg for ten years and during that time, unfortunately I had several miscarriages. I was very sad about this as I always wanted to have children. Soon after,

Richard and I drifted apart and we broke up when Richard became unfaithful and one of his many girlfriends fell pregnant.

Now on my own in South Africa I was aware that I would have to get a job to try and pay for my journey back to Holland. Fortunately I found an apartment in Hillbrow and a job working for Fiat enabling me to save up enough money for the fare home.

The cheapest way was to take a train to Mozambique, then to Lorenzo Marques, (today it is called Maputo) and thence a French charter plane to Paris, from where it would be easy to get a flight to Amsterdam.

It was 10 December 1964 when I arrived in Paris and after an overnight stay in a hotel; I tried to book a taxi to Charles de Gaulle airport. Unfortunately the taxi drivers were on strike and I had to catch a bus to the Airport. On arriving at the airport I discovered that Schiphol airport was closed due to fog and that we would have to land at Brussels. It seemed that everything was against me in my attempt to get home. From Brussels I managed to catch a train to Amsterdam and then jumped in a taxi that took me to Henny's house in Haarlam.

The travel bug was still with me and a few weeks later I saw an advertisement in a newspaper for an au pair in Spring Valley, New York State. I posted off my application and two months later I was off on my travels again. It was May 1966 when mother, Henny, her husband and two children, tearfully waved goodbye to me at Schiphol to catch a flight to the US. Eight hours later I landed at Kennedy International Airport and from there on to Spring Valley where I was greeted by my new family. I spent two wonderful years in the United States but my wanderlust took over again and I decided to go back to Europe.

I was now forty years of age and every day the thoughts of my beloved father were still vivid in my mind; perhaps one day I would visit Indonesia, find his grave and lay a bouquet of white carnations on it. White carnations were his favourite flowers.

I had a friend in Lausanne Switzerland who had offered to try and get me an apartment and a job, so in September 1967 I set off back to Europe on the SS *Rotterdam*. The *Rotterdam* docked in Le Havre

France from where I caught the train to Lausanne where I managed to get a job in a bank. I rented a beautiful apartment with a breathtaking view over Lac Léman and my mother was able to visit me, as it was an easy train journey from Haarlam. Henny, along with her husband and their two children also visited.

Chapter 12

In Search of my Fathers Grave

It was common for the Japanese to take a lock of hair or a nail clipping from a deceased person and forward it to their family, but in my father's case this never happened, there was simply no record of him anywhere. It was now twenty five years since we left the Dutch East Indies and I began the search to try and find his grave. I contacted the Dutch War Graves Foundation who told me that there was no known grave for a Theo van Kampen. His name was in a book that listed 6000 Dutch nationals who had died in the Dutch East Indies without a known grave. I also contacted the Dutch War Foundation but they were not able to supply me with any information. There was simply no evidence of a grave in the name of Theo van Kampen anywhere in Indonesia. Sadly my mother died on the 17th of August in 1987 and I decided to move to Tilburg where I found an apartment, the same apartment I live in today. I wrote letters to the Red Cross and the Dutch Ministry of Affairs in The Hague requesting information about my father's death, but they could not give me any answers. Many questions were haunting me.

Why had the Kempeitai killed him? What had he done wrong? Why was it that he had no known grave? How did he die? Where was he buried? Mother said that he had hidden weapons somewhere in our garden at Sumber Sewu so perhaps that was the reason? The only information I was able to find from the Red Cross was that he died on 25 March 1945 as a political prisoner of the Japanese. I wrote to the '*Moesson'* one of the Indonesian magazines to enquire if they could find anyone who might have known my father and where was buried. I gave my address and phone number but alas there was little response. One gentleman did write to me and told me that he had lived as a boy of ten years old close to the Lowok Waru Kempeitai prison.

'At the end of the war I saw men walking out of that prison, they were completely apathetic, looked very skinny and I knew that they had been tortured by the Kempeitai' he told me.

In July 1994 I received a very emotional phone call from a Mrs Hageman. 'My father was in a cell next to your father; they had brick beds without mattresses and a hole in the floor served as the toilet, the food was extremely bad and the men were regularly tortured in a special torture room. I am sure that your father was still alive at the end of 1944', she told me. 'I think all the men who died in that prison had been tortured or shot and then buried just outside the walls' she added. I was now more convinced than ever that I had to go back to Indonesia and try and find where my father was buried. I wrote to the Dutch embassy in Jakarta requesting permission to visit the prison in Malang where my father was incarcerated but heard nothing. I phoned the National ombudsman in The Hague who told me to write to them with a copy of the original letter I had sent to Jakarta. I was delighted when, several days later I got a phone call from the Dutch Embassy in Jakarta informing me that I would be granted permission to visit the Lowok Waru Prison in Malang.

My friend Agnes and I left Holland on 12 September 1996 bound for the former Dutch East Indies. I could hardly sleep on the flight as I was so excited to be going back to the country where I grew up, the country I have always loved.

It was early morning on 13 September, ironically my father's birthday, when we landed at Medan airport Indonesia. As I stepped off the plane it hit me that it was almost fifty years since I left the country, I was back on the island of Sumatra where my father had brought us 1928. I was completely overwhelmed with the emotion of it all and I burst into tears of joy and sadness.

We stayed in Sumatra for several days before catching a flight to Java. The flight took 50 minutes and as we approached Mahmud Badaruddin 11 airport I got so excited, I couldn't believe that this was really happening to me after all those years - Java was my island. We were met at the airport by a nice young man called Usup, and taken to our hotel, all arranged by our Dutch Travel Agency.

The next morning Usup met us after breakfast to take us to Menteng Pulo, the Allied cemetery for the war victims of the Second World War in Indonesia. This was the cemetery where my uncle Pierre is buried and I was anxious to see his grave. A young assistant was most helpful and led me to the grave whilst Agnes looked around to see if she could find any names on the crosses that she recognised. I stood on my own for what seemed like hours, but in reality was perhaps ten minutes staring down at the simple white cross with the name Pierre van Kampen on it. I felt so lost, sad and empty as the tears trickled down my face. Memories of my uncle's broad smile and cheerful face came flooding back. Was it really fifty five years since I had last seen my dear uncle?

Bending down and touching the cross I murmured 'Farewell dearest uncle Pierre, rest in peace'.
With a heavy heart I made my way across the cemetery to join Agnes who was looking at the rows and rows of white crosses with so many Dutch names on them, all buried so far from home.

The following day Usup drove us to Malang where we had arranged a visit to Lowok Waru prison. As we approached the town I just didn't recognize it at all as it had completely changed from how I remembered it back in my childhood.
We were booked into the Hotel Splendid, a very cosy family hotel just opposite the *'Balai kota Malang'* or town hall, the same hotel where we had stayed as a family for several days in 1936. After checking in we went for a nostalgic walk around the streets where many memories came flooding back. I had found my beloved Malang again; I really felt that I was back where I belonged.

Shortly after breakfast the next morning our driver picked us up and drove us to the prison where my father died. I knew that the visit was going to touch me deeply and I was very nervous. On arrival I handed in the permit I had been sent by the Dutch Embassy in Jakarta. We were given a tour of the prison by one of the guards and I asked him if he knew where my father had died or which cell he had been in. Naturally he wasn't sure which one it was but he showed us a cell which would have been similar to the one my father had been in. The bed was a simple cement slab and the toilet was just a hole in the floor, which during the monsoon season would have been inches deep in filthy water washed up through the hole. A simple bare bulb hung from the ceiling and the guard explained that during wartime this light would have been on twenty four hours a day. My father would probably have slept in his clothes on the concrete slab as there were no mattresses in the cells at that time.

Standing in this damp dismal cell I felt deeply hurt, my father had spent the last years of his life locked up in this 'hell on earth' by the Kempeitai for no reason whatsoever. I just felt so bitter towards the Japanese and it was with deep pain in my heart and my soul that I left the Lowok Waru prison that sunny September day in 1996.

The next day we visited the graveyard in Sukun near Malang, where I thought perhaps my father might be buried. It was a European graveyard before the Japanese occupation and there was a slim chance that I might be able to find his grave.

The graveyard is in a pleasant location with many trees but was quite neglected and overgrown. Agnes and I wandered round for half an hour or so, but as I half expected; there was no sign of any grave with the name Theo van Kampen on it. We called into the small graveyard office where one of the staff was kind enough to look through the many record books and papers, but again they were not able to find my father's name on any list or in any of the books. I was able to tell them that he died on the 25th of March 1945, but that information was of no help.

I left the graveyard with a heavy heart and on the drive back to our hotel I felt completely empty. 'Did my father ever exist?'

The next morning we left Malang at 9.30 and arrived in the village of Dampit just before lunch. It was from here back in 1941, that I took the bus to school early on Monday mornings and where my father would be waiting for me on Saturday afternoons to take me back home for the weekends. The town held many happy memories for me, but of course after fifty five years it had changed beyond all recognition. It was no longer the village as I remembered it but it was now quite a large town with a population of around 23,000.

I was anxious to go back to Sumber Sewu where we lived and to visit the rubber plantation where my father was manager. I knew that it was close to the Ampelgading police station where my father handed over his car to the Japanese in 1942 and I could still feel his grief at losing his beloved car that day.

I was able to tell our driver where to go and soon we were turning into the driveway of our former home. The trees that lined the drive had all disappeared along with most of the house; all that was left was a flight of steps overgrown with weeds along with the ruins of the kitchen, bathroom and toilet. I was dismayed to find the house in ruins. Gazing around I caught sight of the old *Waringin* (Banyan) tree still standing proud and erect. It was still my beautiful *Waringin* tree.

Seeing us arrive, several Indonesians who lived nearby came over to greet us and enquire as to who we were.

'I'm Elizabeth van Kampen and used to live here over fifty years ago' I said proudly.

One elderly man came up to me, took my hands and said: '*Oh, dari tuan* pan Kampen, I often saw you walking over the coffee and rubber plantation together with your father. You were very brave for getting up so early in the morning'.

A nice Indonesian woman, dressed in the old fashioned way with a beautiful blue Kabaya over her Sarong, also took my hands and said: '*Nonni*' (girl) to me. She told me that she was the daughter of our cook Rahima and it was a wonderful moving moment for both of us as we hugged. 'Your mother was a wonderful cook' I told her through tearful eyes. We walked together up the steps and I touched what was remaining of the kitchen wall. 'I can just see your mother standing there' I said to Rahima's daughter.

I gazed over towards the big pond where I used to swim every weekend and every day during my school holidays and the fond memories came flooding back. I could still see the faces of our family friends when they came to visit us, the wonderful food that Rahima prepared for us and the joyful laughter as we all swam in that pond. It seemed like only yesterday. Driving away from Sumber Sewu, I felt sad but very happy that I had been able to visit my old home again.

The next day we set off to try and find the house at 43A Weliran Street, where I was first interned by the Japanese. We quickly found it and I was able to take a photograph for my album. A few streets further on at Lawu street we arrived at my old school where we had arranged for the Principal to show us around. I wanted to see my last classroom again before I had left for the boarding school. The classroom looked almost exactly the same as it was when I left it over fifty years previously.

I didn't want to leave Malang as I knew that my father was buried somewhere in the town, but alas, this was our last day in Indonesia. I knew that it was unlikely that I would ever come back again. Farewell again Indonesia

Chapter 13

Demonstrations in The Hague and Reconciliation in Japan

In 1990, a group of former Dutch Far East Prisoners of War in the Netherlands, set up an organisation called the 'Foundation of Japanese Honorary Debts'. This organisation was set up to look after the interests of those who suffered so badly from the Japanese occupation of the Dutch East Indies during World War Two. The initiative arose from the American Government's decision to pay those Americans of Japanese descent, who were interned during WW2, $20,000 compensation. The group felt that Japan should do the same for the Dutch who were interned by the Japanese Imperial Army in the Far East from 1942 - 1945.

The settlement was a long time in coming and in the eyes of the Dutch it was far from adequate. The United States continually prodded the Japanese Foreign Ministry to give serious consideration to the Dutch request for $250 to each of its 110,000 wartime civilian detainees. A series of internal 1955 State Department memoranda unearthed at the U.S. National Archives, demonstrates how arrogant the Japanese had become in their approach to implementing the agreement. A year later the Dutch government considered submitting a claim to the Japanese government for compensation payment to all victims of the Japanese occupation, but decided against it due to the fact that they (the Dutch) had already reached a settlement on compensation under the 1951 San Francisco Peace Treaty, signed by 48 countries. This decision was opposed by Dirk Stikker (1887-1979), the Dutch foreign minister from 1948 to 1952 and secretary-general of NATO from 1961 to 1964, who refused to waive the rights of his country's citizens to make claims against the Japanese government. He felt that his people had suffered too much loss of life and property under Japanese rule for him to consider such a waiver.

The treaty made no provision for civilian claims and Stikker was adamant in his refusal to sign it on behalf of the Dutch government. As the day for signing the treaty dawned, Stikker was still being the quintessential 'stubborn Dutchman.' The treaty's architect John Foster Dulles, brokered a last-minute agreement that morning and persuaded Japan's Prime Minister Shigeru Yoshida to agree in writing that 'The Government of Japan does not consider that the Government of The Netherlands by signing the Treaty has itself expropriated the private claims of its nationals so that, as a consequence, after the Treaty comes into force these claims wound be non-existent', thus paving the way for the Netherlands to reach a cash settlement with Japan compensating former Dutch residents of the East Indies. The Dutch Government concluded that individual victims could and should make their own claims direct to the Japanese Government and the Foundation was set up to work towards this objective.

In 1994 some individual Dutch citizens started legal proceedings in Japan to obtain compensation based on the Hague Convention of 1907. Unfortunately this was unsuccessful as the Japanese claimed that the 1951 San Francisco Peace Treaty exonerated them of any further responsibility.

It is small wonder then that resentment still smoulders among Dutch survivors of Japanese internment. We consistently refer to our former captors as 'the Japs' and no Dutchman has dared to tell us that this is not politically correct.

I joined the group in 1996 and since then we have continued to demonstrate outside the Japanese Embassy in The Hague on the second Tuesday of every month, when a petition is handed over to the Japanese Ambassador. We usually stand outside the Embassy for about an hour and a half before going for lunch to a local hotel. I also visit the *Indiesch* monument in The Hague on 15 August every year, a monument that was erected by the Dutch government in 1988 to commemorate the liberation of the Dutch East Indies. It is always an emotional visit when I shed a tear and pay tribute to the 8,500 Dutch people who lost their lives during those three and a half years of Japanese occupation. They include of course my beloved father who died at the hands of the Kempeitai a mere four months before the end of the war.

The largest number of civilians interned by the Japanese during their occupation of the Far Eastern countries were of Dutch ancestry.

The Dutch Government paid 5.9 billion Guilders to Dutch citizens who were victimised by the Germans during World War Two, but those of us who from the former colony only received three hundred Guilders each.

For many years we have been campaigning for Japan to compensate us for the sufferings we had to go through during their occupation of the former Dutch East Indies during World War Two. It now seems unlikely that this will ever come about, but as a group we will never give up our demonstrations until we are no longer able to make the journey to The Hague. To this day Japan has never acknowledged that it committed war crimes in the former Dutch East Indies.

Many people died from malnutrition and a variety of tropical diseases due to the sadistic nature of the Japanese military, deaths that could have been avoided by the provision of a decent diet, along with basic drugs that as we know now existed. It was simply inexcusable.

Shortly after celebrating my 73rd birthday in September 2000, a letter came through the post informing me that I had been given a place on one of the AGAPE trips to Japan. AGAPE is a charity set up by a Japanese lady called Keiko Holmes to promote friendship between Japan and her former World War Two POWs. It funds trips to Japan for them in an effort to promote reconciliation.

I was quite excited about the trip, how would I feel about visiting the country of the people who murdered my father? Did I really want to go?

Although Agnes had not been in Indonesia during the war she was also offered a place due to the fact that her father had also died at the hands of the Japanese.

It was May 2000 when Agnes and I set off for Japan with open minds. We arrived in Tokoyo and spent several days taking in the sights of Japan's capital city, before heading to Nagasaki. Of course we were both well aware that this was the city that was almost destroyed by the second atom bomb dropped by the Americans. The last city in the world to ever have had an atomic bomb dropped on it. Nagasaki is the largest city on the island of Kyushu, with a population of 1.2 million and the nearest to the Asian mainland. It is quite beautiful and I fell in love with it right away. We took a tour of the city and visited the Dejima museum, situated on a man made island where the Dutch first stayed when they arrived in Japan in 1638. We visited the peace park and the exact spot where the Atomic bomb fell on 9 August 1945 and were shown photographs of the desolation left in the wake of the bombing. A few days later we travelled across to Japan's main island, Honshu, where we visited the Osaka International Peace Centre. Photographs on display at the centre highlight the horrible devastation that the bomb caused and the effects on the people and infrastructure of the city. I was deeply moved and touched even though I was in the country of the people who had murdered my father.

After fourteen wonderful days in Japan, Agnes and I bade farewell to our hosts and headed home. I left with a completely different perspective about the country and its people, particularly the present generation.

Conclusion

My story started with my beloved father and of course now ends with him. I was sixteen years of age when I last saw him and nineteen when I learnt of his death. Losing him left a deep wound in my soul that has remained with me for the last sixty nine years. Of course I am not alone in my grief, my sisters also lost their father and ninety five percent of Dutch families living in Indonesia lost one or more members during the war period when 170,000 civilians were interned. Ninety percent of those who died in the camps were in the 52 -58 age range and for some reason they seemed to have been the most vulnerable age group. The invasion devastated the futures of thousands of families like ours, who found themselves quickly turned from leaders in the community to virtual slaves. The largest number of western civilians interned by the Japanese in World War II were of Dutch ancestry: people whose families had invested in and cultivated the lands of the East Indies, sometimes for several generations and going back in terms of trading relationships, as far as 300 years.

As we had been an all women camp we had no access to trained administrators, engineers, carpenters, chemists and very few doctors, leaving us very vulnerable. One of the camps in Java that housed over 4,000 women and children had only three doctors to attend to their medical needs. We were lucky in that we only moved once during our imprisonment, but many women and children were moved numerous times by the Japanese usually at very short notice. Often equipment and belongings and equipment had to be left behind and support groups were broken up and women constantly lived in fear of being moved.

An internee of one camp on Java, Daphne Jackson recalls; 'At about two-thirty we moved out of the prison – a most pitiable collection of humanity, covered with ulcers on arms and legs on which the flies settled, and laden with bits of luggage, tins, buckets, and bags. By this time we had learnt to hang on like grim death to any nail, tin or bit of string.'

The journeys between camps, either walking or in trucks and trains, exacerbated health problems and for many people proved fatal. Despite the difficulties, women in the camps displayed an enormous courage and fortitude. The sick were looked after and the dead were buried with dignity. Although they had been dehumanised and defeminised, they found ways of to defy the Japanese and retain their dignity and morale in face of extreme provocation. To make matters worse, the Japanese made several propaganda films to show the rest of the world how well they were treating their 'guests'. Women in some camps were taken to nearby shops where they were given hair makeovers and new clothes. They were then filmed purchasing clothes and food that were then taken off them at the end of the shoot. This was a complete fabrication of what really was going on in the camps at the time.

After the war it was revealed that the Japanese had planned to transport all the Dutch people to the island of Kalimantan, where they intended to unload us onto the beach and sail away. With several thousand miles of coastline and little population, the consequences for us would have been disastrous. Thanks to the American submarine fleet in the Pacific however, they were unable to carry out their cruel plan. The Japanese Government has never fully recognised it's legal and moral responsibility for its crimes committed against humanity during World War Two. Individual Prime ministers Such as Tomiichi Murayma and Kakuei Tanaka, have offered their apologies for the suffering caused by the Japanese military during that period. I certainly feel that these apologies have not gone far enough and that Japan should take the example of the former German Prime Minister Willy Brandt, who in 1970 knelt down at a monument to the victims of the Warsaw ghetto. No Japanese leader has so far agreed to make this kind of apology. Somewhere in the region of 133,000 Western civilians were interned by the Japanese, including some 40,000 children whose only crime was to be living in SE Asia. Fifteen thousand died and those that survived demonstrated incredible courage and adaptability.

Many people have asked me over the years about the time I spent in Banyu Biru 10 prison camp. They are amazed when I tell them that although it was a very hard and miserable time, it has not left me with many scars. The only scars I live with to this very day are the murder of my dear father by the Kempeitai and having to leave the country I was so in love with.

Freedom is a commodity not always appreciated until it is taken away and camp life taught my mother how to fight for survival. She had to stay alive, take care of her children, face the enemy and make far reaching decisions all by herself. Who says that women are the weaker sex? As children we became familiar with death on a daily basis, as we would see people pass away from diseases that could have been prevented. Often those of a similar age who we knew well and had become friendly with. Whilst the Dutch were at war with both Germany and Japan during World War 2, in Holland today people only speak about the German occupation of the homeland. In Britain and America the war against Japan seems to be remembered so much more.

In this book I have tried to set the record straight and offer an insight into the consequences of the Japanese occupation of the former Dutch East Indies. The Foundation of Japanese Honorary Debts still strive to try and get the Japanese Government to acknowledge the atrocities their country carried out in the Dutch East Indies during World War two. When the day comes that I leave this beautiful earth I know that my soul will go back to Sumber Sewu in Indonesia. I will hear my mother play the piano again, I will hear the laughing voices of my sisters playing in the garden, I will eat Rahima's just backed maize-cakes, I will go to the stable and saddle up Trip, my lovely mountain horse, and I will cuddle the adorable doggies and pet the cats. I will talk to Pa Min, our garden boy; I will sit under the banyan tree reading a book as the sun goes down and walk with my father into the jungle. We will once again climb the hill until we can see the Indian Ocean. I will see my father's happy face again and I know I shall be very happy too.

I'm certainly of the opinion that the dropping of the Atomic bombs on Hiroshima and Nagasaki saved my life and those of my family and thousands other people imprisoned by the Japanese. Of course I regret the tragic loss of Japanese lives in those cities and I have seen for myself the devastation caused to families in Nagasaki, but those bombs saved the lives of many civilian and military

Prisoners of War. Had the Americans invaded Japan in a conventional way then many more people would have died.

Had these bombs not been dropped it is very likely that Cecil and I may not have been writing this book today as his father was also languishing in a POW camp on the Thai/Burma railway. President Harry Truman summed it up in his public statement to the American people shortly after the dropping of first the bomb on Hiroshima:

'We have used it against those who attacked us without warning at Pearl Harbor, against those who have starved, beaten and executed prisoners of war, against those who have abandoned all pretense of obeying international laws of warfare. We have used it in order to shorten the agony of the war. Nobody is more disturbed over the use of Atomic bombs as I am but I was greatly disturbed over the unwarranted attack by the Japanese on Pearl Harbor and their murder of our prisoners of war.'

When the Americans began bombing Japanese cities in March 1945, the Japanese people were told that they were a totally 'bestial' enemy. They were never told about the bestiality that we, especially as women and children, in the Dutch East Indies had to suffer at the hands of their military during the previous three years. The Japanese paid particular attention to committing acts of gratuitous slaughter such as that carried out in the Alexandra Military Hospital Singapore on 13 February 1942 when two hundred and fifty patients and staff were brutally murdered in cold blood, many of them on the operating tables.

I recently came across an article written by Sir John Tilley, British Ambassador to Japan from 1926 – 1930 that highlights the Japanese man's perspective during the early part of the 20th Century. He states that;

'In Japan, there is no special courtesy between man and man, and no courtesy at all shown to women'.

As far as women were concerned in Japanese society they were treated as beast of burden to serve the every need of men. Perhaps soldiers raised in the Bushido code thought that guarding female prisoners of war was below them and degrading?

As the war drew to a close in 1945, orders were sent out from Tokyo to all Camp commanders ordering them to dispose of the prisoners of war as they thought fit if the Japanese homeland was invaded by the Allies. A copy of the actual order was found in the safe in one of the camps in Formosa after the war and is from an archive in the US and I will just quote a small section:

'Under the current system, when you take refuge from bomb explosions you must make every prisoner being at one spot under strict caution and kill them all. Method: No matter individually, or in a group, by gas, by bomb, by poison, decapitated, be drowned, choose yourself which suits the occasion. The principle object is "leave no traces". Take every possible means for that.'

In Tokyo between May 1946 and November 1948, twenty eight Japanese war leaders, most of who were class A war criminals, with the exception of the Emperor, were put on trial for war crimes. A further 4,000 were put on trial around the Far East in the class B and C categories.

Over 1000 Japanese camp guards were put on trial in the Dutch East Indies with the first hearings taking place in Batavia in August 1946. Of these, around five percent were acquitted and the rest convicted, with a quarter of them given death sentences. It is interesting to compare this statistic with the Netherlands where only thirteen Germans were convicted of war crimes and all were reprieved.

Most of the Japanese war criminals found guilty but not sentenced to death, were housed in the Tjipinang prison in Batavia for three years, until sovereignty was handed over by the Dutch to the Republic of Indonesia. The remaining Japanese war criminals were transferred to the Sugamo prison in Tokoyo on 26 December 1949 to serve the rest of their sentences. The last Japanese war criminal was released in December 1958. I always wonder if any of the 950 convicted war criminals had been responsible for the death of my father.

Why was it that those of the civilians interned on Java and Sumatra suffered so much worse than elsewhere in the Far East? We may never learn the answer. People have asked me over the years what it was like to feel free again after my internment. The only words I could find to reply to such questions was to say; 'perhaps someone was looking after me, think to yourself: when you are free, water is there at the turn of a tap, bread, butter, beans, milk, eggs, a cup of tea, an aspirin. Deprive yourself of them for even two or three weeks. Add in some bashings and a few deadly diseases. Take away your freedom to speak your own language and do what you like when and where you like. Maybe you might just get a glimmer of what freedom means.

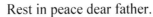

Rest in peace dear father.

Epilogue

After the war ended Holland made a major effort to regain her lost territories in the Netherland East Indies. When the Dutch Colonial Army took over the area, they found around two thousand Japanese soldiers who had stayed behind to help Indonesia gain her independence, still on the island.
During the first nine days of the reoccupation Dutch soldiers brutally murdered two hundred and thirty six Japanese soldiers in retaliation for the treatment they had received in Japanese prisoner-of-war camps. Hundreds who were not killed were interned in slave labour camps in Timor and Java where they tried to recreate the same atmosphere as in the Japanese POW camps. There the Japanese soldiers were tortured and beaten to death when they could no longer work and in a short time the death toll had risen to over a thousand. Those prisoners who survived the retaliation were set free to find their own way back to Japan.
On 10 February 1947 the Dutch government in The Hague declared that it would recognise Indonesian independence and the new Indonesian government met for the first time in Malang on 27 January 1947 ending one hundred and forty seven years of Dutch rule.

If you enjoyed this book why not read 'No Mercy from the Japanese – A Survivors Account of the Burma Railway and the Hellships 1942 – 1945 by the same author

By the laws of statistics John Wyatt should not be here today to tell his story. He firmly believes that someone somewhere was looking after him during those four years. When readers of this gripping memoir examine the odds they will understand why he holds this view. During the Malayan campaign his regiment lost a third of its men. More than three hundred patients and staff in the Alexandra Military Hospital, Singapore, were slaughtered by the Japanese. Twenty-six percent of British soldiers slaving on the

Burma Railway died in captivity. More than fifty men out of around six hundred died on the *Asaka Maru* and the *Hakusan Maru* on their tragic journeys to Japan. Many more POWs did not manage to survive the winter of 1944/45, the coldest in Japan since records began. Yet John survived all these traumatic events and this chronicle of his experiences makes for the most compelling and graphic reading. The courage, dignity, endurance and resilience of men like him never ceases to amaze. Describing as it does with quiet understatement the courage and endurance of his colleagues and the cruelty of their captors, *No Mercy from the Japanese* is a humbling and unforgettable book.

Bibliography

Barber S, *Sadists of the Rising Sun*, Elektron, 2011

Dawes J, *Evil Men*, Harvard, 2013.

De Ruyter Bon K, *As I have loved you*, Covenant, 2003

Edwards W, *Comfort Women*, Absolute crime, 2013

Felton M, *Children of the Camps*, Pen & Sword, 2011

Hillen E, *The Way of a Boy* – a memoir of Java, Penguin, 1994.

Jackson D, *Java Nightmare*, Grafton, 1989.

Krancher J, *The Defining Years of the Dutch East Indies*, McFarland, 1996

Kristensen L, *The Blue Door*, Macmillan, 2012.

Lord Russel of Liverpool, *Knights of Bushido*,

Nitobe I, *Bushido the Soul of Japan*, 1908.

Preisman-Bogaard L, *Dark Skies over Paradise*, Trafford, 2005

Rees L, *Horror in the East*, BBC Books, 2001

Tyrer N, *Stolen Childhoods*, Weidenfeld & Nicholson, 2011

Wolfe I, *Ghostwritten*, Harper, 1988.

Wyatt J, *No Mercy from the Japanese*, Pen & Sword, 2009.

Made in the USA
San Bernardino, CA
27 January 2019